Elite • 141

# Finland at War 1939–45

Philip Jowett & Brent Snodgrass • Illustrated by R Ruggeri

*Consultant editor Martin Windrow*

First published in Great Britain in 2006 by Osprey Publishing,
PO Box 883, Oxford, OX1 9PL, UK
PO Box 3985, New York, NY 10185-3985, USA
Email: info@ospreypublishing.com

Osprey Publishing, part of Bloomsbury Publishing Plc.

Transferred to digital print on demand 2014.

First published 2006
8th impression 2014

Printed and bound by
Cadmus Communications, USA.

A CIP catalogue record for this book is available from
the British Library.

ISBN: 978 1 84176 969 1

Editorial by Martin Windrow
Page layouts by Ken Vail Graphic Design, Cambridge, UK
Index by Glyn Sutcliffe
Originated by PPS Grasmere, Leeds, UK
Typeset in New Baskerville and Helvetica

**The Woodland Trust**
Osprey Publishing is supporting the Woodland Trust,
the UK's leading woodland conservation charity, by funding
the dedication of trees.

www.ospreypublishing.com

**Dedication**
Brent Snodgrass would like to dedicate this book to his family;
to retired Col Heikki Marttinen, who inspired his interest in
Finnish history; and to all his friends in Finland, whose
assistance has been invaluable.

**Acknowledgements**
Many thanks to Harri Anttonen, Sami Korhonen, Jarkko
Vihavainen, Markku Palokangas, the Director of the Finnish
War Museum Helsinki, Vesa Toiven, Jan-Christian Luplander,
Christian Luplander, Stig Jagerskiold, Jyri Paulaharju, Vic
Thomas, Arto Pulkki, Jari Lemmetyinen, Juha Tompuri and
Col Heikki Marttinen, for kindly sharing their research.
Particular thanks go to Marshall Kregal, Lars Oramo, Tero
Tuononen and Alejandro de Quesada for allowing us
generous access to their photographic archives.

**Artist's note**
Readers may care to note that the original paintings from
which the colour plates in this book were prepared are
available for private sale. All reproduction copyright
whatsoever is retained by the Publishers. All enquiries
should be addressed to:

Raffaele Ruggeri,
via Independenza 22,
40121 Bologna,
Italy

The Publishers regret that they can enter into no
correspondence upon this matter.

OPPOSITE
**'Finland's George Washington' – Marshal of Finland
Baron Carl Gustaf Emil Mannerheim, seen here in full
dress uniform. His unique collar insignia displays the
general officers' three gilt lions and his marshal's
crossed batons; at his throat he wears the Cross of
Liberty and the Mannerheim Cross 1st Class – an award
made only to him and to Gen Axel Heinrichs. Born in
1867 when Finland was still part of the Russian Empire,
Mannerheim joined the Tsar's army in 1882 and served
with distinction in the Russo-Japanese War (1904–05)
and in World War I. After the Bolshevik Revolution,
LtGen Mannerheim led the Finnish 'White' army in the
Civil War to defeat Finnish Communists. He was
recalled from retirement in 1933, and in 1939, at the
age of 72, he became Commander-in-Chief of the
Finnish armed forces. Having led the war effort for four
years, he became President of the Republic in August
1944, and steered Finland to peace with the Soviet
Union. He died in 1951, widely mourned as the father
and saviour of his nation. (Alejandro de Quesada
Historical Archives – ADEQ HA)**

# FINLAND AT WAR 1939-45

## INTRODUCTION

Finland, a small Nordic nation of only 4 million people, was almost continuously at war from November 1939 to April 1945. During this period the Finns were actually engaged in three separate and distinct conflicts: the Winter War, fought against the invading Red Army of the Soviet Union from late November 1939 to March 1940; the Continuation War against the USSR, fought alongside the German Army Group North on the Eastern Front from June 1941 to September 1944; and the Lapland War, from late September 1944 until April 1945, fought reluctantly to expel German forces from Finnish territory as a condition of the separate peace with the USSR which Finland's Marshal Mannerheim succeeded – remarkably – in negotiating.

Finland, and her three Baltic neighbours south of the Gulf of Finland – Estonia, Latvia and Lithuania – had only achieved their independence from Russia in 1917–20 in the aftermath of World War I and the Bolshevik Revolution; in Finland's case, independence was

declared in December 1917 but only achieved in May 1918 after a civil war and the expulsion of Bolshevik troops. The Baltic states maintained their statehood as sovereign republics for only 20 years. On 23 August 1939 the Ribbentrop-Molotov pact was signed between Hitler's Germany and Stalin's Soviet Union; this non-aggression pact was to start in motion the reorganization of much of Europe under the control of these dictators, and it specifically assigned the Baltic region to the Soviet sphere of influence.

On 5 October 1939 the Soviets demanded the right to establish military bases in all three Baltic states and in Finland. Additional demands on Finland included the revision of her southern border in Karelia by some 20 miles northwards in the Soviet Union's favour, to create what the Soviets called a 'buffer zone' to protect Leningrad. The Russians also demanded to be granted a 30-year lease for the military use of the Hanko Peninsula, and the ceding of the islands of Koivisto, Suursaari, Lavansaari and Tytärsaari in the Gulf of Finland, along with the Finnish part of the Rybachi Peninsula in

**Finland in 1939–45. Only placenames mentioned in the text are included.**

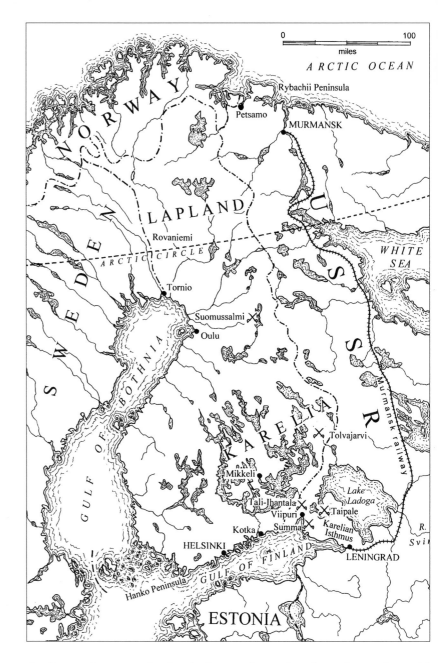

the far north-east on the Arctic Ocean. Accepting these demands would have forced the Finns to dismantle their defences in these territories, in return for which Stalin offered a large but useless tract of wilderness in Eastern Karelia.

While the Baltic nations had little choice but to acquiesce to Stalin's demands, their submission did not save them; in June 1940 all three were re-occupied by the Red Army, and in August they were annexed as 'Soviet Socialist Republics'.[1] Within another year, some 100,000 citizens of these republics had lost their lives at the hands of occupiers who looted, persecuted, executed, and carried out mass deportations in an effort to destroy the conscious identity of these countries forever. Finland stood alone in refusing the Soviet demands, while hoping (vainly) for decisive

This group of Finnish soldiers during the Winter War all wear German M1916 steel helmets, one with a white cloth cover, and white snow coats on top of greatcoats. The tell-tale squared, curled-up toe identifies the Laplander boots. (Philip Jowett Collection)

support from the League of Nations. The Finns were willing to discuss a compromise, but it was clear that the USSR's demands were excessive and cynical. By conceding the areas demanded, Finland would lose the ability to defend herself from future Soviet aggression, which was entirely predictable. Inspired by a patriotic attachment to their long-awaited and hard-won independence, the Finnish people braced themselves for what the Soviet Union and the watching world regarded as a hopeless resistance to their huge neighbour.

# CHRONOLOGY

### 1939

*September–October:* 'Mutual assistance pacts' are signed between the three Baltic states of Estonia, Latvia and Lithuania and the Soviet Union. Finland knows that she is next on the list for Soviet expansion, and begins preparations to resist. Although budget constraints do not allow for any major rearmament programme, the building of new defences begins on the Karelian Isthmus, to increase the number of bunker systems from 168 to 221.

Finland's only significant defences are along the so-called Mannerheim Line (named after the commander-in-chief, Marshal Mannerheim), across the Karelian Isthmus from the Gulf of Finland in the west to Lake Ladoga in the east. This follows a serpentine course of roughly 80 miles through a terrain of forests and lakes.

*9 October:* Finland orders the mobilization of its armed forces.

*11–12 October:* A Finnish delegation meets with Soviet officials in Moscow, and is confronted with a series of unacceptable territorial demands.

*14 October–13 November:* Further negotiations between the Finns and Soviets take place, the former attempting to placate the latter

9 February 1940: two Finnish soldiers lie ready to fire from behind cover. The original caption suggests that they are wearing gas masks because the Soviets were using chloride gas; this was not the case, but would have been useful propaganda in the campaign to attract foreign aid. There were two main types of Finnish-made gas mask; these men appear to be wearing the earlier and less effective m/30 model issued to the infantry, rather than the later m/38 designed for the artillery. (Philip Jowett Collection)

without conceding anything of substance. On 13 November the talks are broken off, and immediate preparations are made for a Soviet offensive against Finland.

## THE WINTER WAR, November 1939–March 1940

*30 November 1939:* The Finnish capital Helsinki is bombed, and Soviet armies totalling some 450,000 men cross Finland's southern and eastern borders at several points. In the south, the Soviet 7th & 13th Armies (Gens Meretskov & Grendal) attack the Karelian Isthmus, with 12 divisions and 7 armoured brigades (120,000 men, 1,400 tanks and 900 artillery pieces), against a defending Finnish force (Isthmus Army – Gen Oestermann) of just 21,600, with 71 artillery pieces and 29 anti-tank guns. North of Lake Ladoga, the Finnish Talvela Group behind the eastern border faces the Soviet 8th & 9th Armies (14 divisions, 1 armoured brigade) on the central front; and on the arctic north-eastern front the North Finland Group (Gen Tuompo) faces the Soviet 14th Army (3 divisions). The Red Army, its command

18 January 1940: Finnish ski patrol moving through a town, wearing the usual camouflage suits. Many Finns were already competent skiers, and the military placed great emphasis on their further training in this type of cross-country movement. Ski troops were well trained for small unit actions, but lack of funds pre-war prevented them from gaining experience of co-operating in larger formations. (Philip Jowett Collection)

The crew of a Finnish-modified Russian Maxim heavy machine gun pictured in December 1939. All wear hooded snow-camouflage suits over their m/36 uniforms; all have different types of gloves, those on the right being Finnish Army issue. Note patches of light-coloured cloth buttoned to the front of their field caps – that on the right even appears to form a pocket? (Robert Hunt Library)

competence weakened by Stalin's disastrous purges of the 1930s, is so complacent that not all the troops committed have even been issued winter clothing

*1 December:* The Soviets proclaim a puppet Finnish Communist government in Moscow.

*3–6 December:* Finnish advanced forces fall back in good order on the Main Line defences.

*6 December:* The Soviets reach the Main Line, and launch the first of several failed attacks. Britain and France decide to send supplies to Finland, but their ability to do so is gravely hampered by declarations of neutrality from Denmark, Norway and Sweden, preventing access across Norwegian and Swedish territories.

*14 December:* USSR expelled from the League of Nations. Widespread sympathy for Finland is expressed in many countries.

*22 December:* After holding their positions on the Main Line the Finns begin a counter-attack, which achieves little.

*29 December:* Successful Finnish counter-attack north of Lake Ladoga against Soviet 8th Army.

## 1940

*7 January:* Soviet Gen Timoshenko appointed to command North-West Group of Forces in Finland.

*8 January:* On the central front, the **battle of Suomussalmi** ends in a Finnish victory. The wooded terrain, cut by frozen lakes and waterways, is under 4 feet of snow, the temperature drops to –40°C, and blizzards prevent most Soviet air activity.

The Soviet 163rd Division begins its westwards advance from the border at Raate to Suomussalmi on 30 November 1939, its dispersed columns harassed by Finnish Civil Guards; it is followed by the 44th Motorized Division. The Soviet force – with a total strength of 48,000 men, 335 field guns, 100 tanks and 50 armoured cars – is attempting to cut Finland in two by a westwards drive to reach Oulu on the Gulf of Bothnia. United at Suomussalmi by 7 December, on the 11th the 163rd Div is attacked by the newly arrived units of the still-forming

**Finnish order of battle, Suomussalmi, December 1939–January 1940**
*Task Force Susi*
Separate Inf Bns 15 & 16
Bicycle Bn 6
2× Civil Guard bns
1× Frontier company
*9th Division (formed 21 Dec 39)*
Inf Regts 27, 64 & 65
Guerrilla Bn 1
Reconnaissance Bn 2
Pioneer Bn 22
Replacement Bn 4
Arty Regt 4 (elements)

*(Total strength c.17,000 men, 11 field guns)*

Finnish 9th Div and surrounded; its supply lines are disrupted, and its units separated into several 'pockets'.[2] An advance in support by the 44th Mot Div is halted short of Suomussalmi on 22 December by Finnish ski troops. Between 24 and 27 December an attempted Soviet breakout from Suomussalmi is foiled and the Finns counter-attack, annihilating the 163rd Div on 30 December. By 8 January 1940 the 44th Mot Div has suffered the same fate. At the end of the battle the booty taken by the Finns includes 43 tanks, 50 field guns, 25 anti-tank guns, 270 motor vehicles, 300 machine guns and 6,000 rifles. Only small detachments of Soviet troops escape from the field, and since only 1,300 are taken prisoner the great majority of the 48,000 men committed are believed to have been killed or to have died of privation.

*1 February:* Timoshenko launches all-out offensive on Karelian Isthmus by 7th & 13th Armies, crossing ice on Viipuri Bay.

*5 February:* British and French governments confirm plans to raise an expeditionary force to aid Finland, but the war will end before anything can be achieved.

*8–11 February:* Heavy Soviet attacks in Summa and Taipale sectors.

*11 February:* Mannerheim Line breached near Summa by Soviet 123rd Division.

*12 February:* The USSR offers, via Swedish intermediaries, to negotiate peace terms with Finnish government. Heavy fighting as Red Army presses on towards Viipuri (Vyborg), supported by massive artillery and air attacks.

*13 February:* Major breakthrough on Karelian front by Soviet 13th Army.

*15 February:* Finnish Army begins to retreat on Karelian front.

*26 February:* The only real tank action of the Winter War takes place; the Finnish tanks are defeated, five out of six being destroyed.

*27 February:* The Finns are forced to give up their second or 'Middle Line' and withdraw to their rear defensive line.

*28 February:* Swedish volunteer force, SFK, is sent to Salla sector of north-central Märkäjärvi front.

*29 February:* Surrounded Soviet force of 3,800 men tries to break out of a pocket in East Lemetti in two separated groups. One group succeeds, the other fails; c.1,500 troops are killed, and the Finns capture 5 field guns, 71 tanks, 12 armoured cars and 206 trucks as well as about 2,000 rifles. The Uudenmaa Dragoons distinguish themselves in this battle, but take very heavy casualties.

**A second lieutenant leads a patrol, 1939/40, mounted on one of the sturdy Finnish breed of horses used by the Army throughout the 1939–45 period – some 70,000 of them during the Winter War, and 60,000 during the Continuation War. The officer wears m/36 winter uniform with the personal addition of a pair of fur gauntlets. His single rose of rank can be seen on his dark collar patch (so not, in this case, cavalry yellow), and on his shoulder strap a regimental badge or national lion emblem. (Marshall Kregal Collection )**

2 See below, 'Tactics'.

RIGHT **Finnish infantrymen, 1939/40, hunker down in a warm shelter which contains many creature comforts. Note the felt-and-leather Laplander boots and the white camouflage trousers. On the left a group of officers are using a field telephone. (Philip Jowett Collection)**

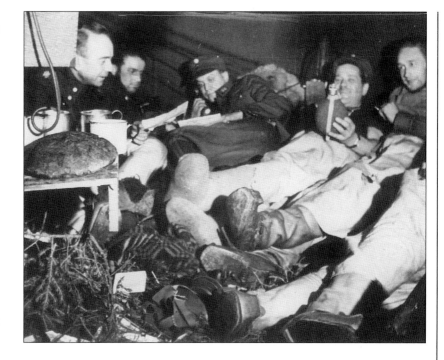

BELOW **Finnish Jaegers pose with the bicycles which provided their transport during summer fighting; they would exchange these for skis when the snow became too deep. The three men in the foreground have fastened their packs to the handlebars, and the soldier on the left has a German M1935 helmet attached to his. They seem to wear straight-cut trousers. (Marshall Kregal Collection)**

*1–12 March:* Heavy fighting continues, and Soviet breakthroughs are achieved in several sectors; sheer weight of numbers is beginning to tell. Finnish defence lines are breached north of Viipuri; the town falls on 8 March, and Soviet troops advance in the Vilajoki and Kollaa sectors. In the Viipuri area the last of the Finnish reserves are committed to the fighting. A Finnish peace delegation leaves for Moscow.

*12 March:* Peace agreement reached; a ceasefire comes into effect at 11.00am on 13 March. Finnish casualties have reached about 25,000 killed and 45,000 wounded, out of armed forces totalling some 300,000, of which 80 per cent are reservists. Soviet deaths in battle and from privation have reached some 200,000, plus an unknown number of wounded which must be least twice as high again. Soviet failures have come as a severe shock to Stalin's regime, and widespread military reforms are planned.

Finland has to cede 16,000 square miles of territory in the Karelian Isthmus, the Salla region on the central front, and in the far north the Rybachiy Peninsula and Petsamo north-east of Murmansk; they also agree to lease Hanko to the Soviets for 50 years. Some 420,000 Finns – more than ten per cent of the total population – lose their homes and have to move to unoccupied parts of the country.

**The interim peace, March 1940– June 1941**

The Finns begin to look for new allies against the Soviets, and find them in Germany. Co-operation between Finland and Germany begins in autumn 1940, and German arms supplies begin to flow. After his lightning victories in the Low Countries and France in May–June 1940 and the thwarting of his hopes to invade Britain, Hitler concentrates on preparing for his long-planned final reckoning with the USSR – Operation 'Barbarossa', set for late June 1941. Early in that month German aircraft begin to arrive in Finland; and on the 22nd they fly from Finnish territory in support of the ground invasion of the Soviet Union.

*25 June 1941:* Soviet bombers retaliate by attacking Finnish military and civilian targets, and a state of war between Finland and the USSR is declared that evening. Finland's objectives are to recover territory lost to the Soviet Union in 1940, and to incorporate a large part of Russian East Karelia into 'Greater Finland'.

## THE CONTINUATION WAR, June 1941–September 1944

### 1941

*29 June:* First Finnish attacks southwards along the Soviet border on the Karelian Isthmus.

*30 June:* The Karelian Army is organized, to begin an offensive in Northern Karelia. This comprises VI and VII Corps and Group O, totalling 5 infantry divisions, 2 Jaeger brigades and a cavalry brigade, with the German 163rd Inf Div from Gebirgskorps Norwegen in reserve.

*10 July:* First major offensive by Karelian Army, which leads to a breakthrough in Korpiselkä area and to the collapse of enemy defences north of Lake Ladoga.

*17 July:* The 1939 border in Karelia is crossed, and the Finns take territory formerly part of the USSR.

*4 September:* Karelian Army launches large scale offensive on Tuulos river.

*7 September:* Finnish advance down Karelian Isthmus is halted near Leningrad. Despite appeals from Hitler, the Finns do not attempt to take the city.

*6 December:* Britain declares war on Finland.

*8 December:* Finland's main war aims have been achieved, with the offensive on the Karelian Isthmus stopping at the old pre-1939 border, just over 6 miles from Leningrad. To the east, between Lakes Ladoga and Onega, the Finns have crossed the old border and advanced as far as the River Svir linking the southern ends of the two great lakes, taking the town of Petroskoi and the isthmuses of Maaselkä and Rukajärvi. With the former Soviet-controlled East Karelia in their hands, the Finns establish defensive positions; Marshal Mannerheim and President Ryti decide not to continue the advance towards the White Sea. The US threatens to declare war if the Finns take the Soviet port of Archangel, which would stop the flow of Lend-Lease supplies.

*29 December:* Finnish losses during this offensive phase of the Continuation War have been 25,475.

## 1942

*1–21 January:* Soviet offensive on the Maaselkä Isthmus, by 6 divisions, 3 marine brigades and 1 ski brigade, against 2 Finnish divisions, 2 Jaeger brigades and 2 independent battalions. The attack peters out without achieving any major objectives.

Throughout 1942 low level fighting continues; its limited scale can be judged by the fact that in June–December 1941 the Finns were losing an average of 464 men per day, but in 1942 only 59 men per day.

## 1943

*12–18 January:* Soviet offensive by Leningrad and Volkhov Fronts clears German troops from southern shore of Lake Ladoga and breaks the isolation of Leningrad, in the same month as the catastrophic loss of German 6th Army at Stalingrad. The Finnish leadership are convinced that the war is lost and that they should try to make peace.

*15 February:* Despite German pressure to take the offensive in order to cut the route for Western Lend-Lease supplies from the north-western Soviet ports, Marshal Mannerheim declares that Finland will undertake no further offensive operations.

*February–December:* The rest of the year sees attempts to mediate some kind of separate peace between Finland and the USSR. American mediation comes to nothing, and Churchill insists that since Finland is an Axis power only unconditional surrender should be accepted.

**A unit of Finnish infantry parade near the 'VKT Line' defences on the Karelian Isthmus in 1943, wearing typical summer uniforms. Their headgear is a roughly even mixture of field and side caps, and their tunics and trousers are in various shades of grey cloth. Nearly all wear high leather boots. Several (e.g. left, foreground) have attached the coloured collar patches from service dress to these field tunics. (Marshall Kregal Collection)**

## 1944

*14 January:* Five Soviet armies of the Leningrad Front (Gen Govorov) – 2nd Shock, 42nd, 67th, 8th & 54th – open an offensive which finally lifts the siege of the city of Leningrad. The Finnish South-East Army (Gen Oesch), holding the Karelian Isthmus, are in a direct line for any new Russian offensive, which is clearly only a matter of time. By June the German/Soviet front line on the Baltic has been pushed westwards to Narva in Estonia.

*9 June:* One of the most intense artillery bombardments of the war opens an attack by the Soviet 21st & 23rd Armies of the Karelian Front (Gen Meretskov) on the Finnish 'VT Line', the frontal defences of the Karelian Isthmus, with the initial objective of Viipuri. The Soviets force the Finnish defenders ten miles northwards up the western shore of Lake Ladoga in a single day, and the VT Line is abandoned on 16 June.

*20 June:* The secondary 'VKT Line' is broken, and Viipuri falls. The Finns hang on north of the city; in return for German assistance, President Ryti is forced to sign an agreement that he will not make a separate peace – which, for the sake of national survival, will be broken.

*21 June:* Gen Meretskov launches a parallel advance by his 7th Army further east, forcing the Finnish Karelian Army (Gen Heinrichs) northwards between Lakes Ladoga and Onega.

*22 June:* The Red Army launches Operation 'Bagration', its massive summer offensive along the whole Russian Front.

*25 June–9 July:* **Battle of Tali-Ihantala.** This monumental battle of attrition, fought in an area of some 40 square miles, is larger in scale than El Alamein, and is to prove the most decisive of the Continuation War – victory will save Finland from the fate of every other country in Eastern and Central Europe.

The main Soviet attacking force is the 21st Army, with a total of 150,000 men in 14 infantry divisions, with tank brigades, artillery, and other heavy support assets. Soviet artillery is concentrated in

Three infantrymen of JR 49 – *Jalkaväkirykmentti 49,* 49th Inf Regt – are pictured in the town of Kivennapa during the Continuation War. This regiment, with JR 7 and 28, provided the infantry of 2nd Division. The officer on the left wears a light overcoat with his m/36 summer uniform; the officer at centre and NCO at right (note the stripe across his shoulder strap) wear the basic uniform. Both the latter have knives at their belts; more often than not these were personal property – hunting knives were popular among the Finns, and were often finely crafted with bone or antler hilts. (Marshall Kregal Collection)

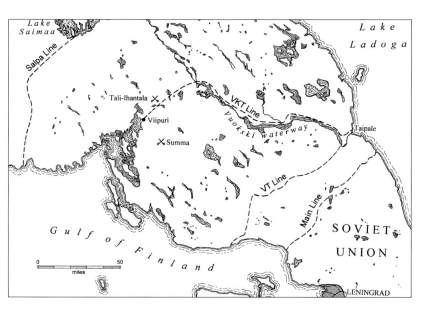

The major Mannerheim Line defences across the Karelian Isthmus. VT Line = Vammelsuu-Taipale, VKT Line = Viipuri-Kuparsaari-Taipale. The Main Line was that built from the 1920s, and defended in December 1939; the others were built during 1941–44. The VT Line was still incomplete when it was hit by the Soviet offensive of June 1944. Over 400,000 cubic metres of concrete were used in more than 900 installations, including tank and artillery positions, mortar and machine gun emplacements, and accomodation bunkers; some stretches were served by railway spurs.

huge numbers, with ten guns every 100 yards, and these lay down some of the heaviest bombardments of World War II. Another Soviet advantage is the terrain, which is well suited to the use of their large numbers of tanks and other armour. Sheer numerical advantage means that the Soviets are – as in 1939–40 – confident of 'steamrollering' the Finns.

Finnish forces total about 50,000 men of IV Corps (LtGen Taavetti Laatilkainen), with 50 per cent of the nation's entire complement of artillery committed to the battle. The main Finnish assets committed at Tali-Ihantala are the 3rd, 4th, 6th & 18th Infantry Divs, the 'Lagus' Armd Div, and the 3rd 'Blue' Brigade. The Finnish artillery perform magnificently, and their accurate fire is one of the main factors in the victory. Another decisive advantage for the Finns is the stark fact that they are fighting not just for their own survival but for their nation's very existence. It has often been said that if the battle had not gone the Finns' way, then every man, woman and child in the country would have come to the front to fight the Soviets.

Soviet planning for the battle is not particularly thorough, and long supply lines to the front delay re-supply of first line units, holding up attacks. Frustrated Soviet commanders often resort to massive frontal attacks, which are skilfully blunted by the defenders. The Finns make good use of their German Panzerschreck anti-tank launchers, and these account for a large number of Soviet tanks – including 25 in one afternoon engagement. The fighting at Tali-Ihantala is as savage as in any battle on the Eastern Front, and losses are severe. The Soviet forces lose between 18,000 and 22,000 killed or wounded, with up to 600 tanks and some 200 aircraft destroyed.[3] In proportion, Finnish losses are even higher: 8,561 killed or wounded. If this battle of attrition had gone on any longer they could not have sustained

This mortar team, about to move up into the front line with their infantry support squad, wear the old 1932-pattern summer uniform with the 1922 version of the field cap. With such large numbers of men under arms Finland's resources were stretched to the limit, and older uniforms and equipment had to be re-issued. Mortar teams were trained to dismantle the weapon, move it up to 200 yards, and then get it back into action all within 5 minutes. (Marshall Kregal Collection)

---

3  At the start of the offensive the Red Air Force on this front had some 1,520 aircraft available; 5 weeks later the figure was 800. The Finns had only about 65 fighters; these pilots claimed 425 kills, and lost ten of their number. See Aircraft of the Aces 23 *Finnish Aces of World War 2.*

such a casualty rate. The whole of the Finnish force fights with great determination and skill, the Jaegers, artillery and armoured troops being particularly outstanding.

Had the Soviet 21st Army been victorious it could have continued north to take Helsinki, and the whole of Finland would have been occupied. The Finnish victory here is to save Finland when peace terms are agreed in September; Stalin has to revise his policy, and decides that a separate armistice should be made with Finland.

*10 July:* The Soviet High Command orders its forces on the Karelian Isthmus to take up purely defensive positions, and the best troops are moved elsewhere to fight against the Wehrmacht. *Stavka* does not need diehard Finnish resistance and a continuing heavy drain of casualties behind the right shoulder of its Leningrad and 1st, 2nd & 3rd Baltic Fronts, as they fight their way westwards into the Baltic states against fierce German and Baltic opposition.

*July–September:* Fighting continues throughout the summer but on a much reduced scale; local Finnish tactical successes do little to change the overall strategic situation.

*1–5 September:* Peace negotiations take place and an armistice is agreed, with an official ceasefire coming into effect at 7.00am on 5 September.

Soldiers photographed during the Continuation War, using a field telephone manufactured in neighbouring Estonia before its annexation by the USSR; Finland had bought most of its military telephones from the Estonians during the 1920s. The Finnish communications systems during the Winter War had been chaotic, however, and additional telephone and radio equipment had been purchased from numerous countries. Note that one man wears a sidecap, the other a field cap; both have summer uniforms, with a buttoned belt-support tab on the left side. (Brent Snodgrass Collection)

## THE LAPLAND WAR, September 1944–April 1945

Finland's separate peace treaty with the Soviet Union naturally leads to conflict with her German former allies, at the behest of the Russians. The Lapland War will be basically a campaign to force all German forces from Finnish territory. On 2 September a demand that they withdraw by 15 September is made by Finnish Foreign Minister Carl Enckell to the German ambassador in Helsinki. All parties know that this deadline is impossible to meet, and that conflict between Finnish and German troops is therefore inevitable; but this is a price Finland has to pay if she is to avoid complete occupation by the Red Army. The Germans for their part have foreseen this rift, as they have been concerned about the possibility of a separate Russo-Finnish peace since as early as spring 1943. German troops have improved and extended the road network in Lapland in case they need an escape route to the Norwegian border.

*7–15 September 1944:* The Finns begin to withdraw civilians from Lapland with German co-operation; the former allies retain a mutual respect, and wish to avoid combat if at all possible. Germans begin to regroup in northern Lapland around the city of Petsamo; 20. Gebirgsarmee are worried about being cut off from the south by possible Soviet and

Three soldiers photographed during the Continuation War while taking 'rest and recreation' – indulging in the favourite Finnish pastime of game hunting; at their feet lies a bear. The man on the right is wearing what appears to be the short blouse usually worn by the Civil Guard in summer. (Brent Snodgrass Collection)

Finnish attacks. The Finns begin to move northwards, hoping that the Germans will withdraw peacefully into Norway.

*13–25 September:* The Finns move 4 divisions and 2 brigades northward. The 15th Bde and the 3rd, 11th and Armoured divisions move into positions in the area of Oulu; the Kajaani–Kuhmo area is assigned to the control of 6th Div and a Frontier Jaeger company.

*15 September:* Germans attack on island of Suursaari in an attempt to gain control of movement on the Gulf of Finland, so that the Soviet Navy will still be blockaded in its northern ports. Fighting between Finnish and German units costs the latter 1,250 casualties, and ends in Finnish success; meanwhile the Germans mine large parts of the Gulf.

*19 September:* Peace treaty between Finland and USSR officially signed.

*27–28 September:* Fighting between Finns and German 20. Gebirgsarmee begins with skirmishes involving Finnish Armd Div at Pudasjärvi.

*30 September:* The Soviets demand full scale Finnish operations against the Germans or they will begin offensive operations of their own.

*1–8 October:* Finnish local commander, LtGen Siilasvuo, attacks German garrison of Tornio on his own initiative; Germans counter-attack, and open warfare breaks out. On 7 September the Soviets successfully attack Petsamo, taking important nickel mining area.

During the Lapland War, winter 1944/45, a group of Finnish soldiers clear mines left over by the Germans – one of the Soviet conditions laid down in the peace treaty. Finnish engineers removed some 31,000 mines, and relatively inexperienced personnel suffered a high casualty rate. (Lars Oramo Collection)

In this blurred but evocative photograph taken during the Soviet 'Great Offensive' of 1944, a tired anti-tank gun crew pose defiantly for the camera; at right foreground is a tank crewman, who may have joined his artillery comrades after his tank was knocked out. Even in the grim situation facing crews like this during the last campaign against the invading Red Army, one or two have managed half-smiles. It was the resistance of men like these that persuaded Stalin that the conquest of Finland would not be worth the cost. (Marshall Kregal Collection)

*October 1944–April 1945:* The Germans gradually withdraw from Lapland, following a 'scorched earth' policy which destroys about one-third of all dwellings in the region. A Finnish attack on the Lap capital of Rovaniemi succeeds, but the Germans leave almost the whole city in ruins. A Finnish attack at Lätäseno in January 1945 defeats the last major German force in Finland and leads to a general retreat. Although small German units remain in parts of Finland until the local end of World War II on 28 April, the fighting in the Lapland War ends in mid November 1944. This campaign against their erstwhile allies has cost the Finns a further 1,000 casualties and the Germans some 2,000.

To this day the Finns regard the Lapland War as an unnecessary conflict, forced upon them by Stalin as an act of revenge.

# ORGANIZATION OF THE FINNISH ARMY

While a rough grouping under the headings of the two main conflicts is helpful, the following material does not separate rigidly between the 1939–40 and 1941–44 periods, and some sections are individually dated.

### THE WINTER WAR

The Finnish Army in 1939 was a well trained infantry force, which in common with most European armies of the period had only a very small armoured and mechanized element. At the outbreak of the Winter War in December 1939 the regular Army had a strength of only 33,000 men – a respectable peacetime size for a nation of only 4 million people. Around this small regular core were a number of territorial and home guard units which could be called upon in time of war, and which would significantly increase the size of the Finnish military.

The most important was the Territorial force, which increased the army to 127,000 men in 9 divisions; additionally there were the Army Reserve, 100,000 strong, and the Civil Guard with another 100,000 men. This total military strength of some 400,000 was further supplemented by the *Lotta Svärd* or Women's Auxiliary Army, a 100,000-strong organization whose members performed support roles which released more men for the front.

**Infantry Division, 1939–40 (14,200 men)**
Division HQ
Supply Co
2× Engineer Cos
2× Signal Cos
3× Infantry Regts (see below)
Light Detachment:
    Jaeger Co (bicycles)
    Cavalry Troop
    MG Pltn
Field Artillery Regt:
    2× field gun bns (each 3× btys)
    1× howitzer bn (3× btys)
Weaponry held by a typical division included 11,000 rifles, 250 sub-machine guns, 250 light machine guns, 116 heavy machine guns, 18 mortars, and 54 pieces of field artillery ranging from 37mm to 152mm.[4]

**Infantry Regiment, 1939–40**
Regt HQ (12 men)
Command Office
Supply Office
Supply Company (169 men)
Supply Pltn (41)
Signal Pltn (55)
Engineer Pltn (45)
Field Kitchen (27)
Regimental Column
3× Infantry Bns

**Infantry Battalion, 1939–40**
Bn HQ (6 men)
Jaeger Pltn
Supply Co (118 men)
MG Co (154 men, 12× HMG)
Mortar Co (83 men, 4× 81mm or 82mm mtr)
    (HQ Pltn, Supply Pltn, + 2× Mtr Pltns)
3× Inf Cos

A soldier of the elite Helsinki White Guards Regt poses for a studio portrait just before the Winter War, in his best uniform with greatcoat. On the tunic's dark blue collar patches and the shoulder straps of his m/36 greatcoat he wears the brass yoke-and-cornsheaf badge of the White Guards, the premier regiment of the pre-war 1st Division, which traced its lineage to the units which defeated the Reds during the 1918 Civil War. (Marshal Kregal Collection)

4 For comparison, a typical contemporary Soviet division had 17,500 men with 14,000 rifles, 419 LMGs, 126 artillery pieces, 40–50 tanks and 15 armoured cars.

**Infantry Company, 1939–40**

Company HQ
Battle messengers (1× off, 1× cpl, 4× men – rifles)
Observer Secn (1× cpl, 3× men – rifles)
Gas Protection Secn (1× cpl, 3× men – rifles)
4× Rifle Platoons, each:
Platoon HQ:
    1× off (pistol &/or SMG)
    1× sgt, 2× messengers (rifles)
2× Rifle Secns, each:
    1× cpl (rifle)
    9 men (SMG + 8 rifles)
2× LMG Secns, each:
    1× cpl (rifle)
    6 men (LMG + 5 rifles)

A mounted lieutenant photographed during the Winter War wears a typical private purchase winter coat with fleece lining; he has added to the sleeves the two silver-grey rank rings from his regulation greatcoat, and side stripes are just visible on his breeches. The cockade on his fleece cap is actually made of pressed paper due to wartime shortages. (Marshall Kregal Collection)

## Cavalry, 1939–45

The small cavalry branch originally had three regiments: the Häme Cavalry Regt, Uudenmaa Dragoon Regt and Karelian Mounted Rifles. A reorganization reduced the establishment to two, with the Mounted Rifles being absorbed by the other two units, which were then formed into a brigade. These elite troops were employed not for mounted combat but as mobile light infantry. During the Winter War each infantry division was also given a 21-man cavalry troop, forming part of the battalion-sized 'light detachment' which also included one company each of bicycle-mounted Jaegers and machine guns.

### Cavalry Brigade, (*Ratsuväkiprikaati*) 1941
(163× offs, 486× NCOs, 3,589 × troopers)
Brigade HQ
Supply Pltn
Signal Sqn
Riding School
Marching Band
Jaeger Bn 1
Häme Cavalry Regt ('HRR')
Uudenmaa Dragoon Regt ('URR')
Horse Artillery Bty
Anti-tank Co

## Jaegers, 1939–45

During the Great War (1914–18) the Germans had recruited Finnish nationals, and in 1915 formed them into the elite 27. Jaeger Bataillon. This was the foundation of a 2,000-strong brigade with small artillery and machine gun units. After the Armistice the veterans returned to their homeland, where they formed the nucleus of the new Finnish Army. Four Finnish Jaeger battalions were formed, equipped with bicycles or skis depending upon the season, and these were widely regarded as the Army's elite units during the 1939–45 period. The Jaegers recruited the fittest and most able men, and soon established a reputation for toughness which led to them being used wherever the fighting was heaviest. As well as acting as 'storm' troops the Jaegers provided many of the long range reconnaissance units during the Continuation War (see below).

### Jaeger Battalion, 1939
Bn HQ
Signal Secn
Supply Secn
MG Co (12× HMG)
Mortar Pltn (3× 81mm mtr)
3× Jaeger Inf Cos (71 men), each:
    Co HQ
    Supply Pltn
    3× Rifle Pltns

## Independent battalions & companies, 1939–40

In the light of the crisis facing Finland in late 1939 a number of smaller non-divisional units were raised to supplement the order of battle.

Twenty-five of these so-called 'separate' battalions were raised in the Finnish-Soviet border region from among the pool of reservists. These ad-hoc battalions – to which others were added during the conflict – were familiar with the localities in which they fought, and although hardly first-line troops they performed well. A further 23 separate companies were also raised: 10 of infantry, 9 bicycle companies and 4 machine gun companies.

### Frontier troops, 1939–45

Finland's long wilderness frontiers demanded surveillance. At the outbreak of the Winter War there were 9 Frontier Companies *(Rajakomppania)* on the Karelian Isthmus and a single 10th Detached Co in the Petsamo region in the far north-east, while 6 Detached Frontier Bns were stationed north of Lake Lagoda.

During the Continuation War all Frontier troops were combined into 8 Frontier Bns and were retitled 'Frontier Jaegers' by Marshal Mannerheim. (Incidentally, the Finnish soldier credited with destroying the greatest number of Soviet tanks with the hand-held Panzerfaust – eight – was Cpl Villi Väisänen of the 2nd Frontier Jaeger Battalion.)

This bicyclist has a typical wartime machine, with a carrying case under the crossbar. He is wearing a lightweight summer uniform – note the shirt-type cuffs. His old m/27 belt buckle plate, of blackened brass alloy, showed the Finnish crowned lion rampant within a laurel wreath. Wartime shortages saw these buckles replaced later with a simple roller-and-claw type. (Marshall Kregal Collection)

### Guerrilla battalions, 1939–43

Guerrilla *(Sissi)* battalions were formed in 1939; each was about half the size of a standard infantry battalion, lacking the HQ company and machine gun company. Five of these battalions were formed during the Winter War from second-line and over-age personnel, and these were quite poorly equipped. As their name suggests they were intended to act more like insurgents than troops, with freedom to attack Soviet targets of opportunity over a wide area. In reality they were used to shore up gaps in the Finnish defences, and were obliged to try to perform the role of standard infantry battalions.

During the Continuation War their numbers were reduced by two, and a third was absorbed into a newly forming infantry brigade as its first battalion. At full strength during the Continuation War a *Sissi* battalion had a strength of just over 1,000 men.

### Foreign volunteers in the Winter War

The 'David and Goliath' aspect of Finland's plight in the winter of 1939 attracted the sympathy of people from many nations, and some foreigners went so far as to volunteer to fight for the Finns, or otherwise aid them. By far the largest foreign contingent came from neighbouring Sweden, which provided nearly 8,760 volunteers during the Winter War. Although about 500 served in various Finnish units, most were formed into the Swedish Volunteer Corps *(Svenska Friviligkaren)*; this SFK had three battalions totalling about 8,260 men, and included anti-aircraft

One of the small number of Estonian volunteers who served with the Finns during the Winter War, wearing a fleece-lined winter coat and an M1916 helmet and armed with a Japanese Arisaka rifle. Since this type of coat was usually privately purchased, it may suggest that this man is an officer. (Marshall Kregal Collection)

and artillery elements. The brigade was formed on Finnish soil, thus avoiding the Swedish government violating the terms of its neutrality, but they did make it very easy for their nationals to get across the border. The SFK was commanded by Swedish officers who had previously volunteered to fight against the Communists in the Finnish Civil War of 1918. In the event the SFK fought for only two weeks, from the end of February 1940, on the quiet northern front, and suffered only 28 killed. The Swedes also provided a vital contribution to the air defence of northern Finland with its Flight Regiment 19, which flew 25 more or less out of date aircraft such as British Hawker Harts and Bristol Bulldogs.

In addition to the Swedes, 727 Norwegian volunteers also served in the SFK. Just over 1,000 Danes arrived, under the command of Col V.Tretow-Loof; and an unknown number of Estonians – the fate of whose country naturally prompted the strongest feelings of solidarity with the Finns. Estonians served in small numbers in the ranks of various units of the Finnish Army, and 56 are listed in 'Detachment Sisu'. This was a unit set up in Lapua to provide training for non-military foreign volunteers; it proved a slow process, however, and by the time the war ended there were only 153 volunteers in the detachment. One group of 346 Hungarian volunteers arrived in Finland as a complete unit after receiving a month's basic training in their home country, and were then sent to Detachment Sisu for further instruction.

Among the other nationalities that came to fight for Finland from further afield were 350 American citizens of Finnish background, who were formed into the Finnish-American Legion *(Amerikansuomalainen Legioona)*. This ASL had two companies; one arrived at the front the same day as the war ended, and only just avoided seeing action. A small group of 13 British volunteers arrived, with a further 214 following a week after the end of the fighting. Another 750 British were waiting in England to go to Finland, and were intended to be formed into a sort of International Brigade under the command of Col Kermit Roosevelt, the son of ex-US President Theodore Roosevelt. In addition, 150 Italians volunteered to fight in the 'anti-Bolshevik' crusade, and one Italian pilot was killed flying for the Finns.

### Artillery organization, 1939–40

During the Winter War there were three basic types of artillery unit: the Field Artillery Regiment, Heavy Artillery Battalion and Separate Artillery Battery. A field artillery regiment was made up of 3 battalions, each of 3 batteries; 2 of these batteries had 76mm field guns and the third 122mm howitzers, each battery having 6 pieces. The total number of pieces per regiment should therefore have been 24 field guns and 12 howitzers, all of which were horse-drawn.

The heavy artillery battalions were under the direct control of the General HQ, for deployment in wartime to the most important sectors of the front. Nine battalions were in existence in 1939, each with 3 batteries of 4 pieces, so each with a theoretical strength of 12 heavy field guns (105mm–107mm) or heavy howitzers (150mm–152mm); in fact, three battalions were under strength.

Five separate artillery battalions had been formed as part of the 'Suojajoukot' Protective Corps, and were intended to blunt the first attacks of an enemy offensive. They were equipped with older light field pieces, and each was intended to have 4 guns, but in fact the 5th Bty had only 2 guns.

### The Civil Guard, 1939–40

The Civil Guard or *Suojeluskunta* (SK) was formed as a separate military organization from the regular Army, but was vital to Finland's defence plans. First raised during the Finnish Civil War of 1918, the SK were really the offspring of the para-military White forces and other pre-Civil War independent military groups. While most of the Civil War veterans went on to serve in the newly formed regular Army after independence, others helped create the Civil Guard.

The SK was a voluntary organization which provided a dual training programme for Finnish youth, initially in a broad range of athletic disciplines and later increasingly in military skills. The national athletic events that it organized promoted an interest in physical fitness, with obvious later benefits for the military. Track and field events and gymnastics were all encouraged, but it was skiing that increasingly became the focal point. The SK even designed its own cross-country skis, which were adopted by the regular Army. While their climate and terrain meant that almost all Finns skied as a matter of course, the added stress on a military technique of cross-country skiing proved to be a critical advantage during the Winter War.

A 76mm light field gun ('76 k/02') just before the Winter War, on exercise in the Perkjarvi training area on the Karelian Isthmus. The Finns had 192 of these ex-Tsarist Russian guns in service at the start of the war, representing about 30 per cent of their entire artillery park. The small defence budget did not allow their replacement with anything more modern. (Marshall Kregal Collection)

Civil Guardsmen, photographed in 1939/40, wearing the brown m/27 uniform (see Plate A1). On the left sleeve of two of them the Civil Guard 'S' arm shield is clearly visible. (Brent Snodgrass Collection)

The SK saw itself as an additional protective force that could be mobilized quickly in the case of an attack on Finland. As the Guard was organized in local units from the same districts they could muster quickly, to slow or halt the advance of any invading force. The Guard's independence from the Army was underlined by its control of separate military stores and weapons repair facilities, and its actual ownership of the famous gun factory SAKO.

From the 1920s the SK sponsored and supported various shooting sports and events. Civil Guard members were the driving force behind Finland's hosting of a world championship shooting competition in the 1930s, and the rifle that won the event was even of SK manufacture, being a Mosin-Nagant m/28–30 from the SAKO factory. Starting in 1929, large scale military training and manoeuvres were sponsored by the Civil Guard. This instruction included not only the use by infantry and cavalry of small arms but also that of machine guns, mortars and artillery, and signals equipment. General battlefield tactics were taught, and even, on a smaller scale, military engineering techniques; the SK membership played a major role in helping to build the various additional fortifications on the Karelian Isthmus which were taken over by the Army in October 1939. These training courses, in parallel with the widespread indoctrination in the importance of marksmanship, were useful in keeping those Finns not actively serving in the Army in a state of readiness. The members of the SK in most cases owned their own rifles and equipment, keeping these in their homes in the same way as the American Colonial 'Minutemen'.

The various programmes and events initiated by the SK allowed Army members and Reserve officers to remain in a high state of training for longer periods, as well as promoting patriotism and a sense of duty. Finland was still a very young nation, which had suffered through a 'White vs Red' civil war in 1918, and was always conscious of the looming might of the USSR over the borders; every opportunity had to be taken to reinforce feelings of national unity, pride and independence.

Despite the Civil Guard's separate identity, many of its members also held rank in the Army, and their Army responsibilities took precedence over their Civil Guard duties; when Finland was mobilized just before the Winter War, these Guardsmen reported at once to their various

Army units. The other members of the SK who were of fighting age were mobilized into Army service; and when hostilities broke out in November 1939 they proved in many cases to be the best equipped, best trained, most steadfast and most proficient soldiers in the field.

Civil Guard membership fluctuated during the interwar period. After reaching 106,900 at the end of the Civil War, throughout the 1920s and 1930s strength stayed fairly level at between 78,000 and 96,000. In 1936 numbers rose to 101,300, and in 1939 to 119,500. These volunteers were to see a great deal of action during the next three years; of the almost 120,000 Civil Guards on strength at the start of the Winter War, a total of about 65,000 saw service in the regular Army. The remaining 55,000 were either too young, too old, or had reserved occupations. Any who were unsuitable for Army front-line service were employed in support and home front duties, but in a few desperate cases front-line units were raised from among these Guardsmen. These included a

Three *Lotta* nurses pose for the camera during the Continuation War. They are wearing the standard grey wool overall dress with white collar and cuffs; note on the left sleeves the *Lotta Svärd* armband. Of white cloth, this had a diagonal stripe of red over black running from top right to bottom left, with a silver embroidered 'S' for Civil Guard centred on it. Above the stripe in black were the words 'Lotta Svärd', and under the stripe the name of the district. (Marshall Kregal Collection)

battalion raised from the Viipuri SK, which acted as a reserve force in the Summa sector of the Mannerheim Line in February 1940. Another example was the formation of seven SK battalions in the Kymenlaakso district to help defend the coast against an expected Soviet attack in the Kotka region.

The importance of the SK to Finland cannot easily be overstated. Their high level of training, armament and equipment was of vital value when the Soviets attacked in November 1939; they provided some of the best Finnish soldiers in the field, and their competence had a calming effect in the front lines. On many occasions their skills allowed them to delay the Soviet advance, buying time for the Finnish Army to regroup. The additional rifle production of the SAKO factory was also significant in keeping Finnish soldiers armed with quality weapons.

### The *Lotta Svärd*, 1939–45

The *Lotta Svärd* organization was founded in 1921 as an unarmed women's auxiliary to work within the Civil Guard. Its female volunteers or 'Lottas' lived by a fairly strict code; this translated as 'The mission of the *Lotta Svärd* organization is to awaken and strengthen Civil Guard ideals and to advise the SK organization in order to protect creed, home and fatherland.' This was to be done firstly by keeping up the general readiness and morale of Civil Guard members, by making and repairing soldiers' uniforms, assisting with medical duties, helping organize rationing and performing general logistic tasks. Other duties included clerical and other office work, and fundraising for the Civil Guard. As the Lottas took over more roles from their male comrades who were fighting at the front, they also performed air raid precaution duties – an often hazardous task that involved manning high spotting towers which were often strafed by Soviet planes.

Three Finnish officers of the postal department are pictured in Lapland with two of their German counterparts. The two Finns at left and centre are wearing the m/22 sidecap with chin strap, while the right hand man wears the m/36 field cap. They seem to wear light summer tunics with winter wool breeches of darker grey shades. Finland's relationship as a co-belligerent with Germany was much more independent than that of the Third Reich's Eastern satellites.

Jaegers move through birch forest during the Continuation War. These lightly armed light infantry units were regarded as the elite of the Finnish Army, and were sent wherever the fighting was heaviest. The number of units was greatly increased over the four pre-war battalions, both by consolidating integral Jaeger subunits from other types of regiment and by new recruitment. (Philip Jowett Collection)

Service in the organization became very popular, and at its peak in 1943 there were over 170,000 members. As was the case with the male Civil Guard (see below, 'Civil Guard Boys units'), there was also a branch for younger members, and these 'Lotta-Girls' numbered almost 50,000 at their peak. During the two wars with the USSR the contribution of the Lottas to the war effort can hardly be exaggerated. They earned the undying affection of the Finnish soldiers, who regarded them as angels who helped make the privations of the war years a little more bearable.

## THE CONTINUATION WAR

In August 1940, after the conclusion of the Winter War, a peacetime organization for the Army was re-introduced: it was to consist of 5 army corps, comprising 12 infantry brigades, 1 Jaeger and 1 cavalry brigade. During the Continuation War of 1941–44 the order of battle would in fact include 16 infantry divisions; these were numbered 1st to 8th, 10th to 12th, 14th, 15th, and 17th to 19th. The only other divisional-sized formation was the Armoured Division, often referred to as the 'Lagus' Division after its commanding officer at all stages of its evolution. (Colonel Ernst Lagus was the first man awarded the Mannerheim Cross on the date of its institution, 22 June 1941.)

In July 1941, Finnish Army strength stood at 495,000 men, which was reduced by autumn 1942 to 376,000 men. The reduction in numbers was due to the fact that the Finns had achieved all their offensive objectives in Russia by this point, and men were needed to help bring in the harvest. By August 1944, when Finland came under the severest Soviet pressure, numbers were increased to an all-time high of 531,000 men. For a nation of just 4 million people, such a figure was obviously completely unsustainable in the long term.

After the 1944 peace treaty with the USSR, Finland's Army was restricted to 34,000 men – comparable to its pre-1939 size. The Navy, of 4,500 men, was restricted to a maximum total tonnage of 10,000 tons, with all submarines to be scrapped. Likewise the Air Force was limited to a maximum of 3,000 personnel, with 60 fighters but no bombers or other offensive aircraft.

### The Civil Guard, 1941–44

By June 1941 the SK had reached a record strength of 126,700 men. During the Continuation War the role of the Civil Guard changed from front-line combat to a home guard type of organization, with responsibilities for local defence and general civil defence duties. Most SK members of fighting age and in reasonable health had already entered the Army; but although no longer a first-line formation the SK still performed a number of important roles, such as anti-aircraft defence, searching for Soviet infiltrators, and organizing the civilian population to perform war duties. SK training centres still provided a valuable resource for the instruction of new recruits for the Army.

LEFT
**Two Estonian volunteers pose outside their bunker, which they have christened the 'Casino'. Both wear either Swedish M1937 helmets or the m/40 Finnish-made copy, and m/36 summer uniforms. The man on the left is armed with an ex-Red Army SVT-40 semi-automatic rifle; these were employed in large numbers by the Finns, who captured well over 10,000 of them. The SVT-38 and SVT-40 were used right through the Continuation War, only being discarded when their actions or barrels wore out. (Marshall Kregal Collection)**

OPPOSITE, ABOVE
**An Estonian volunteer in the Finnish Army is pictured with his military bicycle, wearing typical grey cotton summer uniform with a German M1935 helmet. At least 2,500 Estonian volunteers served Finland during the Continuation War, forming their own regiment, JR 200. (Marshall Kregal Collection)**

OPPOSITE, BELOW
**The cosmopolitan nature of Finnish artillery equipment is illustrated by this photo taken in the 'VKT Line' in 1943. The gun is an '84 k/18' – a US-supplied modification of the old British 18-pounder field gun. The original weapons had been supplied by the UK to the US Army upon its entry into World War I in 1917; the Americans then converted them to fire 75mm French shells, and added pneumatic rubber tyres. Finally, a large batch were sold to the Finns during the Winter War. (Marshall Kregal Collection)**

Since the SK was fervently anti-Communist and patriotic, it was naturally seen as a threat by the Soviet Union, which demanded its disbandment and abolition as a term of the September 1944 peace treaty.

### Civil Guard Boys units

The *Suojeluskunta-pojat* or 'Civil Guard Boys' units gained new importance during the war, as their members were almost the only element of the SK still available in numbers to serve on the home front. Service in these units became very popular among those who were not quite old enough to serve in the regular Army. In 1938 the organization had had approximately 30,000 members, rising to 50,000 in 1941 and 70,000 in 1942. The title was changed in 1941 to *Sotilas-pojat* – 'Soldier Boys' – to recognize their new military role. The soldier boy units received military training, and served in many cases as messengers, anti-aircraft auxiliaries, assistants to the *Lotta Svärd*, and in various other non-combat duties. Members of these boys' units were able to join the Army at 17 years old, when their previous service in the youth corps meant that they could get through basic training faster and into the front line quicker.

### Estonian & Swedish volunteers, 1941–44

During the Continuation War the main group of foreign volunteers fighting for the Finns were the Estonians. Estonia, occupied by the Soviets in 1939, was occupied again by the Germans in 1941, and although many of her nationals chose to volunteer for service with the

Wehrmacht against their Soviet former persecutors, about 2,500 joined the Finnish Army. Under the command of the Finnish LtCol E.Kuusela, they formed *Jalkaväkirykmentti 200* (JR 200), 'Infantry Regiment 200', which fielded two battalions. The first battalion, with 880 all ranks under the command of Finnish Maj E.Kivelä – a Mannerheim Cross winner – was the better trained of the two. These men were on the Karelian Isthmus in June 1944 when the Red Army attacks began, and were forced back to the VT Line after heavy fighting against Soviet armoured forces at Raivola. On 16 June the Soviets broke the VT Line at Kuuterselkä, and this forced the Estonians to pull back to Viipuri Bay. They lost about 26 killed and 150 wounded in this brief but bitter engagement. Most survivors of the regiment returned to Estonia in August 1944, to carry on the fight against the Red Army on Estonian soil.

The other significant group of foreigners serving in the Finnish Army came from neutral Sweden in 1941. They formed the *Svenska Frivilligbataljonen*, 'Swedish Voluntary Battalion', with around 900 men. After being reduced to about half this strength, the hardcore of the SFB was renamed the SFK – *Svenska Frivilligkompaniet* – in which about 400 men served from 1942 to 1944.

### Finnish 'tribal' battalions, 1941–44

Other non-Finnish units were formed in summer 1941 from the Finnish-speaking peoples of East Karelia, initially as two battalions: the Olonets Aunus Tribal Bn (AHSP) and the Viena Tribal Bn (VHSP). A third battalion, designated HeimoP 3, was formed from released Finnish-speaking Soviet POWs and East Karelians who were former Soviet citizens. All three 'tribal' battalions were filled out with Finns, who in fact

A Finnish bicycle soldier sits atop a Soviet BT-7 light tank knocked out during the Continuation War. He has balanced an abandoned Red Army service cap on the gunbarrel – the original caption reads 'The Russian left so fast, he forgot his hat!' Although it looks as if this tank has shed its tracks, the BT-7 was designed to run on good road surfaces without them, directly on the large road wheels of its Christie suspension. Salvaged BT-7s were not used by the Finns in their original form, but the chassis were converted by mounting British 114mm guns donated during the Winter War, to produce the Finnish BT-42 self-propelled gun. Eighteen were built; although ineffective against late-model Soviet tanks they were useful against other targets, and ten survived until 1945. (Marshall Kregal Collection)

made up the majority of their personnel. Both the AHSP and VHSP were well regarded; they fought in the anti-partisan role, and were retitled Separate Bns 25 & 26 in spring 1944. The HeimoP 3 Bn had a less reliable reputation, although reports say that it fought well when in the front line.

### Long range reconnaissance troops, 1939–44

The Finnish use of long range reconnaissance patrols deep behind Soviet lines began during the Winter War, when selected soldiers were trained for clandestine operations. Three detachments of so-called 'Ski

**During the Continuation War, a Finnish armoured unit equipped with Soviet captures advances into one of the towns lost to the Red Army during the Winter War. The lead tank is a heavy KV-1, followed by two T-34/76s – a Model 1943 (left) and a Model 1942 (right). With a tank industry only capable of converting captured vehicles but not of manufacturing them from scratch, the Finns relied on captured vehicles or those supplied by the Germans. (Marshall Kregal Collection)**

**An ex-Red Army Model 1943 T-34/76 tank of the 'Lagus' Division moves up to the front on the Karelian Isthmus in summer 1944. Only six T-34s were captured by the Finns before this date, but the Germans sold them three more. The Finnish-style short-armed *hakaristi* swastika is prominently painted on the glacis plate and turret hatch, in black shadowed with white. (Marshall Kregal Collection)**

A column of German-supplied StuG III assault guns of the 'Lagus' Division photographed in June 1944. The StuG III was one of the most potent weapons available to the small Finnish armoured force, but the Germans sold Finland only 59 of them. Like most Finnish armour from spring 1943, the StuGs are painted in a three-tone camouflage of moss green, mid-brown and grey. Again, note the short-armed *hakaristi* adopted in June 1941 as the Finnish armoured insignia; it long pre-dated the Nazi swastika, being used since 1918 on Finnish aircraft in its original long-armed form. The white number 'Ps531-27' on the front of the superstructure indicates armoured vehicle (ps), type StuG III (531), vehicle number (27). The highest scoring gun in summer 1944, which destroyed 11 Soviet AFVs, was 'Ps531-10', commanded by Lt Brotell of 2nd Company. It bore the white name 'Bubi' on the driver's vision block visor. (Marshall Kregal Collection)

Guerrillas' were formed, and given the designations TO1 to TO3 – from *Tiedustelusasto*, 'reconnaissance detachment'. During the Continuation War these troops were formed into long range patrols to perform not only reconnaissance but also sabotage and other unconventional activities behind enemy lines. Patrols were small, most being only of section/squad or sometimes platoon size; but during the war a few company- and even battalion-sized groups, including specialist personnel such as engineers drawn from other units, were assembled for specific missions.

The personnel of the LRPs were all expected to be at the peak of fitness, and many patrols were made up of young athletes and top-class skiers. They had to endure great hardships during missions that might last for several weeks, and they were issued with 'pep pills' to keep them alert. During 1943, 50 patrols were sent out, and in 1944 just under 100, with various missions including sabotaging the Murmansk railway. One of the most famous of these raiders was Lauri Törni, who led a Jaeger company on so many spectacularly successful raids behind Soviet lines that the enemy put a reward of 3 million Finnish marks on his head (needless to say, this went unclaimed). Attrition rates in Törni's unit were high, and only three of his original men were still alive and uninjured at the end of the war.

### Artillery organization, 1941–45

During the Continuation War artillery unit structure changed little, apart from the fact that a battery could be further divided into two sections. One much-needed reform that did take place attempted to give each unit the same type of field gun – the diversity of types

*(continued on page 41)*

WINTER WAR, 1939–40
1: Civil Guard NCO, Helsinki District
2: First lieutenant, Artillery
3: Reservist, Infantry, 1940

1

2

3

1a

WINTER WAR, 1939–40
1: NCO, Infantry
2: Lieutenant, Infantry
3: 1st Lieutenant, Signals

B

**WINTER WAR, 1939–40**
1: Private, Infantry
2: Sniper
3: 1st Lieutenant, Infantry

1

1a

2

3

**CONTINUATION WAR, 1941–44**
1: 1st Lieutenant, Infantry
2: Private, Infantry
3: NCO, Uudenmaa Dragoon Regt

**D**

**CONTINUATION WAR, 1941–44**
1: Major, Light Detachment, 4th Inf Div
2: Sub-machine gunner, Infantry
3: Corporal, Horse Artillery

E

**FINNISH HOME FRONT, 1941–44**
1: 1st Lieutenant Instructor, Civil Guard
2: Volunteer, Boys' Unit, Civil Guard
3: 1st Lieutenant, Frontier units

2

3

1

2a

**CONTINUATION WAR, 1941–44**
1: Machine gun crewman, Infantry
2: Lieutenant, Transport Corps
3: Lieutenant, Armd Bde/Div 'Lagus'

2

1

2a

3

3a

LAPLAND WAR, 1944–45
1: Private, Infantry
2: Private, Infantry
3: Captain, Infantry

1

2

3

3a

H

in service (see below, under 'Weapons') was obviously a problem. In practice, 11 of the 16 field artillery regiments had their battalions equipped with the same weapons, which made the supply officers' job a little easier. During the 1941–44 period most units were also brought up to strength with more modern field guns wherever possible.

Infantry divisions were also given their own heavy artillery battalion, while those battalions retained under the control of General HQ were motorized. During the Continuation War a new type of motorized artillery unit was introduced known as the Light Artillery Battalion; 15 of these units were raised, each initially armed with 12× 76mm field guns, but they were later re-equipped with new 105mm howitzers. Three Super-Heavy Artillery Battalions were also created, each with 8 or 9 203mm or 210mm pieces, and in 1944 these were each divided into two-gun batteries.

### Armoured troops, 1939–45

Like many of the smaller European nations, Finland had a limited military budget which did not allow for anything more than a token armoured force. During the Winter War the Army had very few armoured vehicles; the single armoured battalion had two companies of obsolete Renault FT-17 light tanks and two of more modern Vickers 6-ton tanks. Only the 4th Armd Co saw any action, and it lost most of its tanks in the fighting. A Separate Armoured Squadron had been planned as an armoured cavalry unit to be equipped with Swedish Landsverk 182 armoured cars; in fact, the single armoured car actually supplied to this abortive unit was the first Finnish AFV to see action.

The large numbers of Soviet tanks which fell into Finnish hands during the Winter War did allow the formation of more armoured units. The 167 captured tanks used by the Finns included 34× T-26, 20× T-37 and a couple of heavy T-28 tanks, and they also captured

A Landsverk II AA tank, one of only six bought from Sweden in 1942 and used by the Armoured Division's AA battery. This conversion of the Landsverk light tank with a 40mm Bofors AA gun was also in service with the Hungarian Army, who called it the Nimrod. (Marshall Kregal Collection)

11× BA-20 and 10× BA-10 armoured cars. Surviving Vickers 6-tonners were also rearmed with captured Soviet guns and were redesignated T-26Es (E = English).

This large acquisition of ex-Soviet armour allowed the Finns to raise an armoured brigade to fight during the Continuation War, and this was expanded into a division in June 1942, with a Tank Bde, the 1st Inf Bde and supporting units. However, the obsolete nature of most of the captured tanks meant that the Finns looked to their German allies to supply them with up-to-date armour, and they did receive limited numbers of modern German tanks and self-propelled assault guns during the Continuation War.

An Assault Gun Battalion was formed in February 1942 as part of the Armoured Division, and was equipped with the BT-42, a Finnish conversion of captured BT-7 tanks with ex-British 114mm guns. In September 1943 the obsolete BT-42s were replaced with 30× German Sturmgeschutz III Ausf G assault guns which the Finns were allowed to purchase; a further batch of 29× StuG III were acquired in 1944. Until July 1944 only the battalion's 1st & 2nd Cos had AFVs, with the personnel of the 3rd Co acting as replacements for the others. Each company was made up of 3 platoons each with 3 assault guns, and an HQ platoon with one gun.

In 1944 the Finns were also supplied with 15× PzKpfw IV, and three captured Soviet T-34s. During the summer 1944 fighting one more T-34/76, 7× T-34/85 and one ISU-152 were captured and employed against their former owners. Heavy losses suffered among the older Finnish-operated Soviet tanks in the 1944 fighting led to General HQ ordering all T-26, T-28 and BT-42 to be withdrawn from combat use, but the armistice with the Soviets forestalled this. Despite heroic individual efforts, the handful of Finnish tanks were to make little impact when faced by Soviet forces equipped with huge numbers of more modern types.

# TACTICS

In December 1939 it was obvious that in a straightforward confrontation the Finns, with their army of less than 130,000 men before reserves had been mobilized, their few hundred artillery pieces and their handful of old tanks, had no chance against the invading Soviet juggernaut with 450,000 men, 2,000 guns and about 2,000 tanks. This huge disparity in numbers and weaponry was, however, partly offset by the generally superior skills and flexible tactics of the Finnish Army.

Although the invading Soviet armies in the Winter War did contain some good units the majority of the men, drawn from the Leningrad Military District, were patchily-trained conscripts, and some were literally raw recruits. From senior commanders down to unit level, the officer corps had been gutted and cowed by the murderous purges of the 1930s, which robbed the Red Army not only of experience but also of initiative in command. The Finns were to exploit their one real advantage to the full, employing ingenious and daring tactics. Born of necessity, these expedients were to inflict heavy losses on the invaders, even though in the end the sheer weight of numbers against them prevented her defenders from saving Finland from defeat.

In this atmospheric photograph, a patrol of Finnish ski troops move off across a clearing in the forest during the Winter War. They presumably wear only minimal equipment – belts and ammunition pouches – under their snow smocks. Three carry Mosin-Nagant rifles, and the leader seems to have a slung sub-machine gun. Such troops were very much more mobile than the Soviet infantry, and used this advantage to the full to off-set the Soviets' huge preponderance in numbers. (Robert Hunt Library)

The Finns were, in the main, fit, rugged, independent countrymen, motivated by love of their young nation. This fitness and motivation had been encouraged and harnessed by good training in the Civil Guard and regular Army alike. They excelled in marksmanship, and few troops in the world could match their skill in small unit tactics. Their tactical doctrine stressed the value of bold initiative and decisive leadership. For the most part the Soviet officers and NCOs showed little initiative, mostly through fear of failure and consequent punishment – even execution. They relied upon superior orders no matter what the consequences, and rapidly lost momentum when faced with tactical obstacles.

### 'Motti'

As the long columns of Soviet armour and other vehicles advanced into Finland along narrow single-track roads through the snowbound forests their rate of advance soon slowed, and they became bogged down. This left the columns strung out over long distances, with small groups of vehicles becoming isolated, and thus open to attack. Sometimes the head of the advancing column would be attacked by Finnish troops and the rest of the vehicles would stop and adopt static defensive positions. Once the column had stopped it immediately became vulnerable to a Finnish envelopment tactic which came to be known as 'Motti'. This Finnish term literally means a cubic metre of cut timber, and has long been used in Finland as a measurement for firewood; its use for encircled Soviet troops – *Mottiryssä* or *Motti-Russki* – carried the sinister implication of 'firewood just waiting to be burned'.

More often than not, the *Motti* tactic was not part of a pre-planned doctrine; it was simply a Finnish adaptation to the opportunities they were offered by the behaviour of Soviet troops under fire. The term had not even been used in a military sense before January 1940, when the Finnish IV Corps first coined it, but it soon caught on. Only one *Motti* was fully planned from the start – a much larger than usual operation at a place called Kitilä, which trapped the Soviet 168th Division.

Normally the Finns attacked the weakest of the trapped Soviet units first, further isolating the stronger and less vulnerable pockets. Often the Soviet positions were too strong for the Finns to overrun, in which cases they relied upon pin-prick attacks to keep the Russians fixed and off-balance, while the very severe winter weather took its toll. The poorly-clothed Soviet soldiers got little sleep, and never knew when the next attack would come. The biting cold sapped their will to resist, and thousands simply froze to death at their posts. Meanwhile the warmly-clad and well-camouflaged Finns moved from one Soviet position to another, attacking them at will and then disappearing into the forest.

The Finns found that the best way to destroy the Soviet pockets was to harass the Russian soldiers for at least 24 hours, depriving them of sleep, warmth and food. Then the Finns would attack with fast strike teams on skis, armed with sub-machine guns, grenades, 'Molotov cocktails', satchel charges and smoke grenades. They would often infiltrate into Soviet lines before opening fire, sowing further confusion. Once sufficient damage had been done the Finns would quickly move off to attack another *Motti* before the Soviet troops had a chance to regroup. Any attempt to break out of the pocket was usually blocked successfully; the Soviet troops' reliance on their vehicles hampered them in trying to manoeuvre their way out of encirclement.

## Snipers

Finland fielded some of the best snipers of the World War II era, and many Finnish snipers achieved kill ratios that seem almost unbelievable. Sniper training in Finland was not on a massive scale, but such instruction as was given was to a high standard. As already mentioned, both the Civil Guard and the Army had long stressed the importance of marksmanship, and this helped to produce a number of extremely successful snipers.

The most famous was a man called Simo Häyhä, who served in the 6th Co of the 34th Inf Regt in the heavy fighting on the Kollaa river during the Winter War. Before the war Häyhä had served in his local Civil Guard unit, quickly becoming renowned for his skill with a rifle. He took this training to war against the USSR, and

Simo Häyhä, right, was called up for the Winter War and served with *Jalkaväkirykmentti* 34 on the Kollaa river facing the 9th and 14th Soviet Armies on the eastern front. Known for his quiet disposition and good nature, he became one of the most lethal snipers the world has ever known, with more than 500 kills. Here he wears a hooded snow smock over the m/36 field cap and greatcoat, and felt-and-leather Laplander boots. Neither of the two rifles he holds here have telescopic sights – remarkably, he was known for preferring the 'iron sights' to which he had always been accustomed. The officer at left wears the m/22 fleece cap with two badges. (We are grateful to the Häyhä family for permission to reproduce this photograph.)

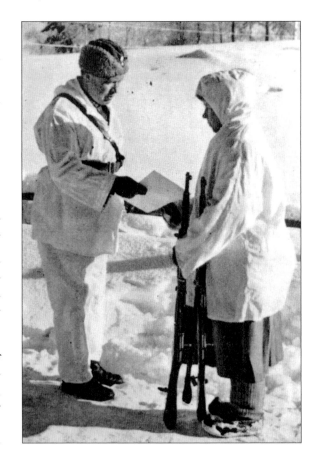

achieved more than 500 kills, with both his rifle and a sub-machine gun. Almost incredibly, these kills were achieved in a mere 100 days' fighting, since he was wounded in action on 6 March 1940 when struck in the face by an exploding bullet.

Before the Winter War the number of scoped sniper rifles produced in Finland was extremely low, with only a few examples of M1891, m/27, m/28 and m/28-30 weapons being fitted with optical sights. Their use became more common during the 1939/40 conflict as captured examples of Soviet Mosin-Nagant rifles fitted with PE and PEM sights became available; but even then, most Finnish sharpshooters preferred to keep using their standard 'iron' sights.

# WEAPONS, 1939–45

Throughout the 1939–45 period the Finns used a wide variety of small arms and other weapons imported from all over the world. This eclectic mixture of weaponry was usually forced upon them by circumstances, but it is an interesting aspect of this particular World War II combatant army, and is worth the space for a brief examination. (In series style, most date designations are given in the standard form e.g. M1936; those for Finnish designs are expressed as e.g. m/36; and local Finnish designations of foreign designs are given as e.g. 'm/36'.)

### Pistols

Although the lack of standardization was a problem common to all weaponry, it was particularly acute with respect to the issue of handguns, and led to considerable logistic difficulties; luckily, of course, the handgun had little real significance on the modern battlefield. There were pistols in 9mm, .380 ACP, .32 ACP, 7.65mm and 7.62mm calibres, among others. Some of the more common types in use were old Russian Nagant revolvers, Soviet TT-30/33 semi-automatics, the Czech CZ series, Belgian FN-Browning M1935 'Hi-Powers', various Italian Berettas, Spanish Rubys and Astra 300s, and Mauser M1896 'broomhandles', among a great many others. As in many armies of the period, officers purchased their own pistols, which added to an already chaotic situation.

These front-line soldiers photographed during the Continuation War are armed with a representative mixture of infantry weapons: from foreground to background, a Lahti LS-26 light machine gun, a Mosin-Nagant m/27 bolt-action rifle and a 'war booty' SVT-40 semi-automatic rifle. The two men in the foreground wear Finnish m/40 helmets, and the soldier in the background an Italian M1933. (Tero Tuononen Collection)

18 September 1941: a Finnish
soldier poses on the track of a
destroyed Soviet tank, holding a
captured SVT-40 semi-automatic
rifle. (Marshall Kregal Collection)

The single most important pistol in Finland before 1939 was the 9mm German P08 ('Luger'), mostly brought back to the Finnish Civil War by former members of the German 27. Jaeger Bataillon. After 1918 it was selected as the standard sidearm of the Finnish Army, but since the Treaty of Versailles forbade the production of 9mm weapons in Germany, during the 1920s the Finns ordered 8,000 Lugers in 7.65mm from the German firm of DWM; these were designated 'm/23', and were widely used by both the Army and the Civil Guard, some of them issued with a detachable shoulder stock like the 'artillery Luger'. In 1940 a small number of 9mm Lugers were imported from Belgium and designated 'm/08' by the Finns, who also manufactured some 9mm barrels during the Continuation War.

The most famous Finnish handgun was a semi-automatic designed by Aimo Lahti, the L-35. A robust and well-made 9mm pistol closely resembling the Luger which it was meant to replace, it never reached its full potential due to severe production delays and budget problems, and the Luger remained the standard sidearm until 1945.

## Rifles

In 1919 the new Finnish armed forces urgently needed to decide on a standard issue rifle to replace the heterodox mixture of Russian, German, Austrian, Italian, French, British, American, Japanese and other weapons carried in the Civil War. With over 190,000 Russian Mosin-Nagant M1891 rifles and large amounts of 7.62mm ammunition stockpiled from the inventory of the former Russian garrisons, the choice was not difficult. In the 1920s Finland began a programme of disposing of other types while procuring Mosin-Nagants from nations including Germany, Poland, Bulgaria and Czechoslovakia. The stockpiled rifles were both issued and used as a source of parts for

Finland's own Mosin-Nagant production, which both the Army and the Civil Guard had begun by the mid 1920s. The latter produced the m/24 Civil Guard rifle, and the former the m/27, which ushered in a long line of excellent Finnish versions of the Mosin-Nagant. A carbine version of the m/27 was also produced in the 1930s, but since its issue was limited to mounted troops total production was less than 2,200 units.

By the mid 1930s the parallel production of rifles for the Army and Civil Guard was judged unacceptably wasteful, and after trials the m/39 was developed for issue to both Civil Guard and Army, with production beginning in 1940. However, the production volume fell short of the needs of greatly enlarged defence forces, and in the same year manufacture of the old M1891 rifle was resumed. Those produced in 1940–43 were much as the earlier 1920s production, though with new stocks and sling swivels. There was also limited production of a copy of the Soviet M1891/30 during 1943–44, but only some 5,000 were made by the end of 1944.

All the Finnish-made Mosin-Nagants were a great improvement on the Tsarist/Soviet models, with newly designed barrels, replacement sights, and in many cases newly designed stocks. With the exceptions of the M1891 and m/24 they shared only the receiver, bolt and magazine with their Russian-made counterparts. The Finnish rifles were manufactured to a much higher standard, and could achieve the greater accuracy which Finnish marksmanship demanded. However,

In a hastily dug position, two Finnish soldiers are armed with a Suomi kp/31 sub-machine gun and a captured Soviet Degtyarev DP light machine gun; the gunner's Mosin-Nagant rifle is propped against the snowbank at the right. Both men are well protected against the cold and well camouflaged, including white cloth wrapped around their field caps. (Robert Hunt Library)

they were never available in sufficient numbers, and Finland still had to rely upon Tsarist/Soviet-made rifles right up to 1945. The original Russian M1891 was the most common weapon at the end of the Winter War, and was still a mainstay during the Continuation War. Even such older designs as the venerable 'Russian Winchester' M1895 saw limited issue in 1939–45. In 1940 Finland also purchased 77,000 Swedish M1896 Mausers and 94,000 Italian Carcano M1938 carbines. These non-standard calibre weapons were mainly issued to home guard, field artillery and anti-aircraft units.

During the Winter War the Finns also captured two new Soviet types: the fully-automatic Simonov AVS-36 and the semi-automatic Tokarev SVT-38. Only some 300 examples of the AVS-36 were taken, and while these were issued and used their overall contribution was minimal – they were notoriously unreliable. The Tokarev SVT-38, which had once been intended to become the new standard Red Army rifle, was first issued to Soviet troops in any numbers during the Winter War. It was rather well liked by the Finns, who had no other semi-automatic rifles in service and valued the SVT-38's additional firepower; by the end of the Winter War they had captured some 2,700 examples. In the 1941–44 campaigns the Finns captured more than 15,000 semi-automatic rifles, most of these being the improved Tokarev SVT-40, which also proved popular.

A nice study of a Finnish ski trooper wearing a white smock over a roll neck sweater. His kp/31 sub-machine gun is slung around his neck and spare 70-round drum magazines hang from his belt. (Philip Jowett Collection)

### Sub-machine guns

The first sub-machine gun used by the Finnish Army was the 7.65mm Bergmann 'm/20', a German design manufactured in Switzerland, which was used by the Civil Guard from 1922. Eventually they had about 1,400, most of which were transferred to the regular Army at the start of the Winter War; during the Continuation War they were handed on again, to coastal and home defence troops.

One of the best weapons in the Finnish arsenal was the 9mm Konepistooli kp/31 sub-machine gun, more widely known as the Suomi ('Finland'). Developed from 1930 by Aimo Lahti, the kp/31 was bought by the Civil Guard to replace their Swiss-made Bergmanns, and the Army also placed orders in 1931. It was originally issued with a 20-round box magazine and a 40-round drum, the latter being replaced in 1937 with a 70-round version. Well made, rugged, and reliable even in extreme conditions, the Suomi may have been the best SMG in the world, and became the iconic Finnish weapon of the Winter War. Only 4,000 were in service in December 1939, but they proved so effective that production was soon given priority, and by June 1944 more than 60,000 had been manufactured. During the Continuation War a new two-column 50-round 'stick' magazine was produced, and in 1942–43 a muzzle brake was added. There were also 'bunker' and 'tanker' models, which had different lengths, barrel shrouds and stocks.

The kp/31 was apparently nicknamed 'White Death' by Soviet soldiers, and even influenced Red Army policy. Before the Winter War Soviet SMG production was limited, and only modest numbers of the PPD-34 and PPD-34/38 were in use; experience during that conflict demonstrated the true potential of such weapons, and by the end of World War II the USSR had become the world's most prolific producer of sub-machine guns, with over 3 million made.

As the numbers in service in 1939–40 were so low only a few hundred examples were taken by the Finns. During the Continuation War they encountered Soviet SMGs in much greater numbers, and by the close of hostilities they had in their inventory several hundred PPD-40s, over 4,000 PPSh-41s, and approximately 5,000 PPS-43s. As these took non-standard ammunition most were issued to rear area troops. A Finnish copy of the PPS-43 was also made by Tikka, the m/44; a small test batch in that year was followed by a 10,000 production run in 1945.

### Machine guns

The standard heavy machine gun in Finnish service throughout the 1939–45 period was the classic water-cooled Maxim design, of which a number of models were used. Two were Russian versions, left over from 1918 or bought from various sources in the 1920s: about 100 examples of the M1905, and some 400 of the M1910. By 1944 the Finns had over 4,000 Soviet Maxims in service, including various anti-aircraft versions. The other major Maxim variants in use were the 'm/09-21' and 'm/32-33', which were basically 1910 Maxims with Finnish modifications including an improved tripod and feed system. The m/32-33 also had improved cooling: a large hole was cut in the water jacket, allowing both quick refilling with water and also the use of snow as a coolant – an effective modification that was later copied by the Soviets.

**Finnish recruits train with the Suomi sub-machine gun while their instructor and fellow trainees look on. The kp/31 was a very well made weapon which operated efficiently in the extreme conditions faced in Finland, though it was expensive to manufacture. The officer with his hands on his hips appears to be from the Civil Guard, and wears the old brown m/27 tunic with a paler sidecap. Experienced Civil Guardsmen were often responsible for this kind of training on behalf of the regular Army. (ADEQ HA)**

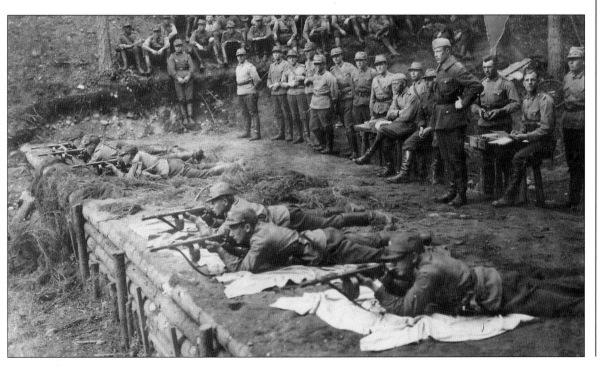

There was also limited use of German MG08 Maxims, mainly by coastal artillery or other second line units. The Soviet M1939 Degtyarev DS and M1943 Goryunov SG were among several other types of MG used in limited numbers.

**Light machine guns** in Finnish service were also of several types. The first Finnish-designed arm was the 7.62mm Lahti-Saloranta LS-26, of which the first batches were completed in 1929–30; this was fed by 20-round magazines. Under battle conditions in the Winter War this weapon proved to be a little too well made, being manufactured to such fine tolerances that dirt often caused stoppages. The Finns found captured Soviet LMGs much more durable, and their key type thus became the standard Degtyarev DP. By the end of the Winter War Finland had captured and put into use more than 3,000 DPs, and by 1944 over 9,000 examples. The tank version, the DT, soon became the main MG seen in Finnish tanks, and its infantry adaptation was also in service.

Other LMGs used by the Finns included the Swedish 'm/21', the Belgian FN M1930 and the venerable Lewis. French types seen during the Winter War included the very unreliable M1915 CSRG 'Chautchat', and 100 of the much superior Chatellerault FM24/29. A number of Danish Madsen 'm/20s' acquired between 1921 and 1936 were still in service.

## ANTI-TANK WEAPONS

When the Finns were attacked by the largest army in the world in November 1939, one of the major threats they faced was Soviet tanks. The Finns had never faced tanks in battle before; they were unprepared both tactically and psychologically, and they sorely lacked anti-tank weapons.

In this photo, dated 8 January 1940, an anti-aircraft machine gun crew at Salla on the north-eastern front man a modified Russian-made Maxim M1910 fitted with AA sights. The Finnish 'm/32-33' modification had a booster that allowed two rates of fire, the faster rate mainly used in the AA role. The crew appear to wear fleece-collared coats under their camouflage clothing. Operating weaponry in the extreme cold was difficult unless the correct gloves were worn: bare skin would quickly freeze to the metal. (Philip Jowett Collection)

In their extremity, the Finns employed any field piece that could loosely be described as an anti-tank gun; these included a handful of ex-Russian 37mm infantry guns – the M1914 'Obuhov' and M1915 'Rosenberg' – captured in 1918. Both were totally unsuitable for the anti-tank role and were soon withdrawn. The first true anti-tank gun purchased by Finland was the 37mm Swedish Bofors M1937, which was designated '37 k/36'; 48 examples had arrived by the beginning of the Winter War, and the Finns also concluded a licensed-manufacture agreement for both the State Artillery Factory (VTT) and Tampella. Tampella had an order for 100 guns in 1938 and another 100 in 1939; but due to production problems they had completed only 46 guns by October 1939, and by the end of that year VTT had produced only 48 pieces.

A Maxim 'm/32-33' heavy machine gun photographed in thick woodland during the Continuation War. The men are all wearing summer uniforms, but the fact that the gun still retains some of its winter whitewash suggests that the photograph was taken in the spring. This model of the Maxim series was the Finnish Army's standard heavy machine throughout the 1939–45 period. (Tero Tuononen Collection)

The 37mm m/36 was a well-made AT gun, although that calibre was fast becoming obsolete in 1939–40. The low numbers available during the Winter War obliged the crews to move quickly from one firing position to another, which is in fact best practice for AT guns. Despite the shortage not only of guns but also of ammunition and trained crews, the Finns performed well against the Soviet tanks and armoured cars then in service. Other AT guns that arrived in Finland during the Winter War were the Danish 20mm Madsen 'Pst k/40' – which was in fact found to be much more suitable in an AA role; and the French Hotchkiss 25mm 'Pst k/34' and 'Pst k/37', of which 40 were delivered in February 1940. The Finns also captured and used over 100 various 45mm Soviet AT guns.

By the start of the Continuation War the k/36 was out of date, and thereafter it was mainly used against fixed Soviet positions such as bunkers and MG emplacements. During 1941–44 Finland possessed a much greater number and assortment of AT guns than in the Winter War. In total she received 463 German guns: 200× 37mm Pak 37 and Pak 40, 27× 50mm Pak 38, 46× 75mm Pak 97/38, and 190× 75mm Pak 40. By September 1944 the Finns had also captured a further 550 Soviet 45mm AT guns with plentiful ammunition.

## Anti-tank rifles

In 1939 a number of nations still regarded AT rifles as a viable class of weapon.[5] It was only in September 1939 that a prototype 20mm weapon, designed again by Aimo Lahti, was approved by the Finnish Army; this was to become the L-39, a gas-operated semi-automatic with a ten-round magazine. Only two examples reached service during the Winter War, being issued to the AT platoon of JR 28 in the Lake Ladoga region. They performed very well; despite their considerable weight they were still mobile with a two-man team, and very accurate. During the

A Finnish soldier takes aim with his domestically produced 20mm semi-automatic Lahti L-39 AT rifle, with a top-mounted ten-round magazine. The Lahti could be fitted with a four-legged support with sledge-shaped feet for use in snow, as here. Only two examples were ready in time for the Winter War, but many more by 1941. Outdated against the later Soviet tank types, they continued to be used to break up fixed positions, and even in some cases as long range sniper rifles. For these additional roles a variety of rounds were produced, including a phosphorus incendiary that was particularly hated by Soviet soldiers. A fully automatic version was also designed for AA use, designated the L-39/44. (Tero Tuononen Collection)

Continuation War L-39 production was increased and more than 1,800 were fielded. While the 20mm round was ineffective against the later Soviet tanks it remained deadly to more lightly armoured vehicles and useful in other roles.

During the Winter War 100 British Boys .55 AT rifles were donated, and another 300 were obtained during the Continuation War. Other foreign types used in 1941–44 included 30 examples of the 8mm Polish 'm/38' and 12 Swedish 20mm Solothurns. An unknown number of captured Soviet 14.5mm PTRS and PTRD weapons were also used.

### Mines

The Finns designed their first AT mine in 1936; this m/36 was of disc shape, with a jagged bottom which allowed it to be placed firmly in snow or ice. The first charges used proved too weak; among the responses was the practice of using two mines in tandem. The m/36 was also difficult to use and rather over-complex; but the replacement m/39 was not available in time for the Winter War, as production did not get underway until December 1939. The new mine in fact shared many of its predecessor's shortcomings, and two simplified versions were quickly produced. These ms/39 and ms/40 models were both contained in simple wooden boxes; much easier to produce, they were also more 'soldier-friendly' in the field. By the end of the Winter War more than 125,000 had been manufactured, and many were put to good use in the heavy fighting of the closing stages of the war.

In the Continuation War a number of AT mines were acquired from Germany, including the TMi41, TMi42, TMi43 and TMi44 versions of the highly effective Tellermine. Cleared Soviet minefields also brought the Finns reusable munitions; and in their major defensive lines – such as the VT and Salpa Lines – the use of such assorted mines added to their security. The Finns also used against tanks a number of expedients that were not designed for such use but still proved effective. One was the so-called 'glass mine', which was simply a bottle filled with explosive.

These were placed in groups on the ice of frozen lakes and rivers threatened by Soviet armoured assaults; their detonation would break up the ice, plunging the tanks and any accompoanying infantry into the icy waters. Remotely-detonated TNT charges placed under the ice achieved the same results.

### Satchel charges & 'Molotov cocktails'

To make up for the shortage of conventional AT weapons the Finns used their undoubted ingenuity to devise or improve upon a number of improvized expedients. In World War I the Germans had used wired-together bundles of 'stick' grenades against French and English tanks. In 1936, Finnish Capt Kaarlo Tuurna decided he could improve upon this; he found that a correctly placed 0.5kg (1.1lb) TNT charge could penetrate 12mm of armour, and he proceeded to design satchel charges for issue to Finnish troops. Known as *'Kasapanos'*, these were usually very basic, consisting of a TNT charge packed inside a sheet metal box, combined with a wooden handle and a fuse system much like that of a stick grenade. The handles and fuses varied from charge to charge, as different factories had their own systems; indeed, many versions were also produced by soldiers in the field, thus adding to the range of variation. The factory-made charges were produced in three sizes ranging from 2kg to 4kg (4.4 to 8.8lb) of TNT.

**The crew of a Bofors 40mm AA gun photographed some time during the Continuation War. Note the very characteristic summer use of the lightweight pale cotton summer tunic with darker grey winter wool trousers and caps; examples are illustrated on Plate C. A Bofors crew consisted of an NCO and seven men; an AA section had two guns plus an additional AA machine gun team, and a total of 30 men including observation and supply teams. (Philip Jowett Collection)**

A Finnish crew clean the barrel of their captured Soviet 45mm AT gun in the shade of a fir tree during one of the summers of the Continuation War; they are pushing the cleaning rod through the barrel from the breech end. This gun, based on a scaling-up of the 37mm German PaK 36, was a welcome if slightly obsolescent addition to the Finns' inadequate anti-tank armoury. (Marshall Kregal Collection)

The Finns produced many thousands of these charges in the Winter and Continuation Wars. Although they could be damaging weapons, their weight made them difficult to throw accurately. They usually had to be thrown from very close ranges, aiming for the tank's tracks or engine deck. In many cases they were used in combination with the most famous of the Finnish improvized AT weapons, the 'Molotov cocktail' – a glass bottle filled with flammable liquids, with a simple hand-lit fuse, which was thrown to break on a tank.

The first widespread use of this type of weapon against armour was during the Spanish Civil War, but it was the Finns who jokingly christened it after Stalin's foreign minister. Its introduction was preceded by propaganda from Finnish Army HQ, saying that a new 'secret weapon' was on the way to destroy the Red Army tanks that were wreaking havoc in the Finnish lines. The man who developed the version seen in Finland was Capt Eero Kuittinen, the commander of an Army pioneer company. When the 'cocktails' were first produced a number of mixtures were used, but the recipe which became most popular was 60 per cent potassium chlorate, 32 per cent coal tar, and 8 per cent noulee. The ignition systems also varied: some used the classic kerosene-soaked rag, others a friction match system, and later, more advanced versions a breakable sulphuric acid capsule that ignited the liquid on impact.

The first tactical use of these new weapons was to be in conjunction with satchel charges; it was hoped that the 'cocktails' might blind or disorientate the crews, allowing men with satchel charges to get close to the tank. It was later discovered that if the bottles broke on the rear engine grill they would ignite the fuel vapour inside. This form of attack became standard, and many Soviet tanks were destroyed with these primitive and inexpensive weapons. During the course of the Winter War a total of about half a million 'cocktails' were produced. They became a symbol of the Finns' fight for survival: to use them effectively required great courage.

(While the 'cocktail' may have been primitive, it must still have come as a Godsent improvement over some earlier techniques employed against armour. These desperate, almost suicidal measures included attempting to pry the tank tracks off the sprocket or idler wheels with a crowbar, or immobilizing tanks by jamming a heavy log into the tracks.)

## Panzerfaust and Panzerschreck

In the greatest possible contrast to such methods, in April 1944 the Germans supplied the Finns with their first examples of a revolutionary new generation of infantry AT weapons – the Panzerfaust and Panzerschreck anti-tank launchers.[6] Over 1,500 Panzerfaust-kleins and 300 Panzerschrecks were delivered in preparation for the expected Soviet summer offensive. The Finnish training with these weapons was very limited, however, as their expected arrival had been kept secret from most of the Army, and most Finns fired their first shots with them in the heat of battle rather than on training ranges. Luckily the Panzerfaust was reasonably easy to use and the Finns were quick learners, but the men using them still suffered heavy casualties.

This lack of training was evident when, in June 1944, the Red Army launched their massive armoured assault up the Karelian Isthmus. In that same month the Finns had received the improved Panzerfaust

The crew of an ex-Red Army 45mm AT gun in action under fire during the Continuation War. The Finns had captured 125 of these weapons during the Winter War alone and many more after June 1941, with a peak number of 670 in service at one time. Gun crews suffered very heavy losses during the last defensive campaign of summer 1944. (Philip Jowett Collection)

6 See Elite 124, *World War II Infantry Anti-Tank Tactics*

Summer 1944: an anti-aircraft crew prepare their camouflaged 20mm 'It k/35', an Italian Breda AA cannon. Finland had a total of 92 of this type in service, some arriving during the Winter War and others in the intermediate period before the outbreak of the Continuation War. The crew, which normally consisted of six men, wear a mixture of sidecaps, field caps and a German M1935 helmet. (Marshall Kregal Collection)

30 version (though only after assurances to Germany that Finland would not pursue a separate peace). The Finns did not receive the later Panzerfaust 80 or Panzerfaust 100 versions, and the overall success of this weapon in Finnish hands is debatable. Soviet tanks and SP guns encountered in 1944 had thick armour, which the Panzerfaust 30 did not always penetrate. In all more than 25,000 Panzerfausts were sent to Finland in 1944 but, significantly, only 4,000 were used in combat. The Panzerschreck, in contrast, was very successful, and was used with outstanding results in the heavy fighting of summer 1944. The teams issued these weapons were usually of three men: one firer, one ammunition carrier, and one to provide covering fire with an automatic weapon. After the Soviet breakthrough on the VT Line in June 1944 many of these teams laid in wait to buy time for the regrouping units, and their actions played a major part in allowing the Finnish Army to retreat in good order to the VKT Line. Approximately 1,800 Panzerschrecks and at least 18,000 rocket rounds were delivered to Finland by the end of August 1944.

While the anti-tank weapons available to them were of uneven quality and quantity, overall the Finns were quite successful in repelling or destroying Soviet armour. In the fighting of June–September 1944 the Red Army lost almost 600 tanks on the Finnish front, of which only a small proportion fell victim to Finnish armour. This high attrition rate was partly due to the Finns making good use of tank traps and obstacles; they were helped by the fact that much of Finland is not well suited to tank movement, and large areas of the Karelian Isthmus are thickly wooded and cut by many water obstacles.

### Artillery

Finland used a staggering variety of artillery pieces during the 1939–45 period, acquired from every conceivable source by purchase, donation or capture. As in many other combatant armies, the Finnish artillery branch was initially reliant on old weapons. During the Winter War the most common type was the ex-Tsarist Russian 76.2mm M1902

('76 h/02') light howitzer. Another Russian howitzer which had been in Finnish service in modest numbers since capture in 1918 was the 122mm M1909 and M1910 ('122 h/09, 122 h/10'). Finland sought to buy artillery from any source possible, and – largely due to international sympathy for her plight – she received guns from the USA, UK, Belgium, Spain, France and Norway. Unfortunately, most of these were elderly pieces no longer required by their owners, and most did not arrive before the end of the Winter War. Some of these older pieces were used by the Finns during the Continuation War, many being issued to the fortress and coastal artillery.

The Finns captured large numbers of Soviet artillery pieces during both their wars against the USSR, and most were put into service during the Continuation War. These included 86× 76mm M1936 ('76 k/36'); 125× modernised 76 h/02, designated '76 k/02-30'; and 41× 122mm M1938 howitzer ('122 h/38'). About 70 other guns purchased from various countries during the interwar years were in service in 1941. During the Continuation War a number of Soviet-modernized examples of the M1909-1910 howitzers were captured ('122 h/20-30'); this led to the Finns up-dating their own pieces and giving them the designation '122 h/10-40'.

Newer artillery introduced during 1941–44 included 103× Finnish-made 105mm howitzers (105 h/37), and 53× German 105mm M1933 howitzers ('105 h/33') received in April 1944. Sweden sold Finland 64× Bofors 105mm M1934 field guns ('105 k/34') for coastal artillery use, but in 1942 these were transferred to the field artillery. Bigger guns in Finnish service included 48× German 150mm M1940, purchased in late 1940; and 4× 210mm M1917 bought from Sweden during the Winter War, and used for bombarding fortified positions.

**Two Finnish artillerymen wait to get their ex-Soviet 122mm howitzers (h/10-30) into position during the Continuation War. The Finns had captured 35x 122mm field howitzers during the Winter War, and these came in two slightly modified versions. Both the h/09-30 and h/10-30 had strengthened carriages and were able to take more powerful ammunition; the h/09 also had a muzzle brake fitted. (Marshall Kregal Collection)**

**Artillerymen training in the use of a German rangefinder during the Continuation War. All are wearing the winter m/36 uniform; the two men in the foreground have reversed their field caps so that the peak (visor) will not get in the way when they use the optics. The soldier on the right has the two stripes of a junior sergeant on his shoulder straps. (Marshall Kregal Collection )**

# THE PLATES

While many of these illustrations show field dress, the basic service dress and insignia of the regular Army should be described. The drab grey uniform worn during 1939–45 was introduced in 1936, replacing the brown M1927 (m/27) service uniform. The m/36 tunic was single-breasted, with exposed buttons and four patch pockets with buttoned pointed flaps. It was worn with breeches by all ranks, those of NCOs and officers with one and two light grey stripes respectively. Straight-cut, undecorated trousers were also issued, and were widely worn by all ranks during wartime. The headgear were an m/36 peaked (visored) 'mountain' or 'ski'-type field cap, with a cloth peak and folding side/rear flap, or a sidecap of m/22 pattern, fitted with a chin strap. Pre-war officers' and senior NCOs' caps and shoulder straps were piped in arm-of-service colours (see below). Officers wore a 'Sam Browne'-style belt.

Circular national cap badges/cockades were generally worn. For regular Army officers the badge was ruby-red with a gold edge, and bore in gold the national lion symbol – crowned, rampant, wielding one curved sword in its paw and trampling on another. For enlisted ranks the badge was a cockade in national colours, white/light blue/white; this was of painted metal for troops and enamelled for non-commissioned officers. On the sidecap two badges were sometimes worn by NCOs and officers: the national cockade, above a white metal button bearing the lion symbol for NCOs, and above the gold-on-red lion badge for officers.

The arm or branch of service was indicated by coloured collar patches. These were edged with a contrasting frame – a simple inset edging for enlisted ranks, and with fir-twig motifs inside the front corners for officers. Junior officers and captains wore a single frame, field officers a double frame, and general officers a narrow inside a wide frame. The main arm-of-service colours were as follows, all with silver grey framing unless otherwise noted:

General Staff – light crimson
Guards – dark blue
Infantry – green
Jaegers – green, with gold/yellow frame
Cavalry – yellow, with blue frame
Artillery – red, with black frame
Coastal Artillery – black, with red frame
Engineers – purple
Signals – purple, with yellow frame
Armour – black, with orange frame
Service Corps – medium blue

Rank symbols were displayed on the collar patches in yellow metal. NCOs from corporal to senior sergeant wore one, two, three or four narrow chevrons pointing forwards, and sergeant-majors a single broad chevron. Junior officers from second lieutenant to captain wore from one to three roses, and field officers from major to colonel one to three slightly smaller roses. General officer ranks wore from one to three national lion emblems. On greatcoats, officers wore light grey cuff rings: one to three, narrow, for lieutenants and captains, and the same below a single wide ring for field officers.

The NCO rank chevrons were also worn on the shoulder straps, points inwards, inside arm-of-service symbols and unit numbers; some pre-war units wore particular badges instead. Officers wore the national lion on the outer end of the shoulder straps, sometimes with special unit badges. Arm-of-service symbols were worn on the greatcoat shoulder straps by all ranks. The main arm-of-service symbols were as follows:

Infantry – crossed rifles
Jaegers – bugle horn
Cavalry – crossed sabres
Field Artillery – flaming bomb
Heavy Artillery – crossed flaming shells
Coastal Artillery – crossed cannons
Engineer officers – sword and cogwheel
Signals – sword and crossed lightnings
Technical, Signals & Service troops – sword and cog over crossed lightnings.

Two others seen during wartime were those of Light Detachments – bicycle wheel and crossed skis; and Frontier units – bear's head, sword and fir twigs.

In 1939–45 a wide range of commemorative unit, divisional, front, and other breast badges were devised, often of handsome coloured designs, but these were hardly ever seen on field uniforms – though various proficiency badges were.

Field uniforms were much plainer than service dress, with a shorter, fly-fronted tunic on which only the breast pocket buttons were exposed; a light cotton summer version was also worn. The officers' roses and lions of rank were pinned directly to the grey collar; NCOs wore their chevrons, or simple transverse stripes, only on the shoulder straps.

When the field uniform was worn as service dress the coloured collar patches were added, and arm-of-service symbols or unit badges were often pinned to the shoulder straps.

## A: WINTER WAR, 1939–40
### A1: Civil Guard NCO, Helsinki District HQ

This Civil Guardsman from the Helsinki district is wearing a tunic of the obsolete brown wool m/27 pattern; but although the trousers are in the same shade they are cut to a straight-leg m/36 pattern. He displays the Civil Guard badge (fir twigs above 'S' for *Suojeluskunta*) on his left sleeve, the diagonally-divided white and blue background specifically identifying Helsinki District; other districts wore the same badge with different colours, e.g yellow and black for Mikkeli District, white and red for Häme District, etc. The two bronze badges on his breast pockets are individual proficiency badges. The *Hakaristi* or 'short' swastika on the collars has no connection with the Nazi symbol, being a national emblem seen in various Finnish insignia and awards; in this case it identifies SK staff NCOs. **(See insets for details of all these insignia).** His magnificent boots are the high-leg version of traditional 'Laplanders', with the soft upper legs folded down; this 'Lapland' foot shape was very widely worn by the Finnish Army. The helmet is a German M1916, one of the most common types in service during the Winter War. His field equipment is basic: a waist belt supporting two triple pouches of German World War I pattern, carrying ammunition clips for his 7.62mm Finnish-made Mosin-Nagant m/28-30 Civil Guard rifle.

### A2: First Lieutenant, Artillery

This young officer wears standard m/36 winter uniform, with a pre-war field cap (note red artillery piping) and officer's badge. His privately purchased tunic has brass buttons, and displays the collar patches of his branch and rank, but no insignia on the shoulder straps. A pair of m/36 straight-leg trousers are tucked into officer's high boots. On his Sam Browne belt he has a Finnish-made holster for a small calibre semi-automatic pistol.

### A3: Reservist, Infantry, 1940

As a reservist called up in the latter stages of the war this man is wearing what was commonly referred to as the 'Cajendar model' uniform – in other words, his own civilian clothes; this nickname came from the surname of the then Prime Minister of Finland. His cap, trousers, coat and home-knitted sweater are sturdy and practical, as are his Laplander boots, here of mixed leather and felt construction. On arrival at the front he has been issued with German World War I ammunition pouches, worn two at the front and three at the back. The only insignia that most men wearing civilian dress

LEFT **A Civil Guard looks towards the Soviet border just before the outbreak of the Winter War. Although they are not clear in this photo, he wears the Civil Guard shield on his left upper sleeve, above what appear to be two NCO chevrons, and a proficiency badge on his left breast pocket. (Marshall Kregal Collection)**

RIGHT **A young enlisted man of JR 3 – 3rd Inf Regt – during the Winter War. This shows clearly the m/36 winter tunic, with pleated breast pockets, and the grey-framed green collar patches of the infantry. His m/39 fleece cap bears the enlisted man's painted metal version of the national cockade, and he wears an m/30 belt with a simple brass roller-and-claw buckle. (Marshall Kregal Collection)**

**Winter 1939/40: a Finnish officer in a rather extravagant but practical fur coat prepares to fire a flare pistol. Behind him, a brother officer has wrapped his m/39 fleece cap in white cloth to match his smock. (Brent Snodgrass Collection)**

could hope to receive would be a national cockade ('*Kokardi*') badge to pin to their headgear. Besides his personal hunting knife he is armed with a Swedish Mauser M1896 rifle; this, and its carbine version, saw some use by the Finns in 1939–40.

## B: WINTER WAR, 1939–40
### B1: Sergeant, Infantry
This fairly young NCO is wearing a pre-war m/36 tunic with unusual white shoulder strap piping, showing that at the outbreak of war he was attending Reserve Officers School – white was the colour of that training academy. His pre-war m/36 breeches have the NCO's single sidestripe, and are worn with Laplander boots. His helmet is another example of the eclectic mixture used in Finland during 1939–45 – an Austro-Hungarian M1916 Berndorfer. His minimal equipment is a knife and a single German World War I ammunition pouch for his Russian-made Mosin-Nagant M1891 rifle. **(Inset:)** collar patch.
### B2: Lieutenant, Infantry
Officers were often on close terms with their men; as units usually came from the same district, they knew most of them by their first names. This typical privately purchased m/36 tunic is worn with an m/39 winter cap, breeches bearing the double stripe for officer's rank, and high-leg officer's boots. The Finnish-made holster worn on the Sam Browne belt holds his Mauser M1896 'broomhandle' semi-automatic pistol.
### B3: First Lieutenant, Signals
Like his brother officer B2, this lieutenant is wearing an m/36 tunic, with the purple rank patches of the Signal Corps on the collar, and the branch badge on his shoulder straps. His m/36 straight-leg trousers are tucked into boots made of black felt and leather. The m/39 winter cap is made from non-standard black fleece, but displays the standard officers' badge on the front. He is unarmed, but carries a canvas equipment bag. **(Inset:)** branch badge.

## C: WINTER WAR, 1939–40
### C1: Private, Infantry
This young soldier is wearing a typical uniform of the Finnish patrols which constantly harassed the Soviet invaders during the winter campaign. The hooded snow-camouflage smock is worn with an m/39 winter fleece cap over wool m/36 uniform; such smocks were often home-made from bed sheets. White camouflage gave the Finns a great advantage over the Soviet troops, who had been sent into Finland wearing their standard khaki uniforms. Again, he wears high Laplander boots, a very practical form of footwear which had evolved for exactly the conditions faced by the armies during the Winter War. His Mosin-Nagant M1891 rifle is complete with a scabbarded bayonet; tucked into his belt is a French-made flare pistol for use during a night attack. At his feet is a simple anti-tank satchel charge of TNT incorporating a stick-grenade type handle.
**(Inset:)** Enlisted ranks' and officers' national cap badges.
### C2: Sniper
Finnish snipers took a heavy toll of Soviet troops, especially of their officers, thus reducing the leadership of surrounded units to an even lower level of initiative. This sniper wears a complete white camouflage suit of hooded jacket and over-trousers over his fleece cap, wool uniform and Laplander boots, probably with as many other layers of clothing as he can lay hands on. Knitted items such as socks, gloves, head-warmers and scarves were donated by the Finnish public; and note his heavy mittens, taped around his neck. He is travelling light, with only a canvas 'bread bag' to carry food and spare ammunition. The Mosin-Nagant M1891 rifle is fitted with a Soviet PEM telescopic sight, one of two captured types in use during the Winter War; but even with their basic 'iron' sights, there were confirmed kills by Finnish snipers at ranges of over 500 yards.
### C3: First Lieutenant, Infantry
Shortages of every necessity during the mobilization and expansion of the Finnish Army in 1939/40 required a high degree of improvization and personal initiative. This company officer wears a privately purchased winter cap and sheepskin winter coat (note partial cuff rings) over his m/36 uniform, with straight-leg trousers and high officer's boots. He has a slung canvas map case, and his Sam Browne belt supports the holster for his German 'm/23' Luger pistol.

## D: CONTINUATION WAR, 1941–44
### D1: First Lieutenant, Infantry
During the winter campaigns of the Continuation War the Finnish Army wore more or less the same m/36 uniform as worn by the majority of soldiers during the Winter War. This infantry subaltern's tunic is worn with straight-leg trousers and Laplander boots, and the m/39 winter cap with the officer's red-backed lion badge. He has armed himself with a captured Soviet Tokarev SVT-38 semi-automatic rifle, for which he carries two spare clips in the pouch on his Sam Browne belt. Other equipment that he has acquired includes a pair of English-made binoculars, and a Finnish-manufactured torch worn on his breast pocket.
### D2: Private, Infantry
From head to foot he wears standard m/36 wool uniform, including the field cap with the enlisted ranks' cockade, and enlisted ranks' black leather boots. His equipment is a mixture of Finnish and ex-Russian items, with a home-

Group of Finnish junior officers outside their headquarters during the Winter War. They wear a mixture of m/22 and m/39 fleece caps; note (left, & front centre) the m/22 with its V-shaped gap in the turn-up flap, displaying the national cockade on the cloth crown – the m/39 had the badge pinned to the frontal flap. Some of these officers (see left) seem to wear the m/36 grey tunic with black breeches from a pre-war regular officers' and senior NCOs' private purchase walking-out uniform. (Marshall Kregal Collection)

produced water bottle and rucksack and Russian World War I ammunition pouch. He is armed with a superior Finnish-made m/39 Mosin-Nagant rifle, a knife, and a captured Soviet M-33 stick grenade. (Inset:) collar patch.

## D3: Sergeant, Uudenmaa Dragoon Regiment

Cavalry troopers were often selected for their slight build, and this NCO is smaller than average. His m/36 wool tunic and breeches are worn with the distinctive m/22 pattern fleece cap favoured by this regiment, with an NCO's enamelled cockade; his boots are also the special cavalry issue. The cavalryman's equipment is made up of a leather

belt with Finnish-made 'Y' straps and a German World War I vintage ammunition pouch. The m/27 cavalry carbine was only issued to mounted troops. Both cavalry regiments were employed as elite mounted light infantry strike forces, and moved rapidly around the battlefront. The URR was among the first units to be hit by the Soviet offensive on the VT Line in June 1944; they saw the very hard fighting there, further north at Viipuri Bay, and later in Ladoga Karelia at Ilomantsi, the last battle of the war; by the ceasefire they had suffered devastating casualties. (Inset:) collar patch.

## E: CONTINUATION WAR, 1941–44
### E1: Major, Jaegers 4th Light Detachment, 4th Infantry Division

This major serving in the elite 'Kev Os 4' detachment is wearing officer's m/36 summer combat uniform with its special shoulder strap badges (inset), and his German M1935 steel helmet bears the white skull emblem of light detachments; several variations on the basic design are known. On his belt are a German-made holster for the 'm/23' Luger, and a hand-made knife with reindeer-bone handle in an ornate leather scabbard. He also has a map case.

### E2: Sub-machine gunner, Infantry

Troops on the Karelian Isthmus had this extra top tab and button, allowing the tunic collar to be worn open. The official scale of issue of sub-machine guns in 1939–40 was to one of the ten men in each rifle section, and to one of the seven men in each LMG section. During the Continuation War many more SMGs became available, by issue or capture; this man carries the excellent Finnish Suomi kp/31, and the small silver badge he wears on his left breast is the SMG proficiency pin (**inset**). Typical m/36 summer uniform is worn with felt-and-leather boots. This m/40 Finnish steel helmet was worn concurrently with the German M1916 and M1935 models, the Austro-Hungarian M1916, Czechoslovakian M1934 and Italian M1933 – in fact, with so many types of imported helmets in service it is rather surprising that the Finns bothered to produce one of their own. His equipment is limited to a 'bread bag' to carry magazines and small kit; as well as his personal knife he has acquired an ex-Soviet M-32 stick grenade, and may have others in the canvas bag.

### E3: Corporal, Horse Artillery

The summer-weight m/36 tunic bears the red collar patches of this branch; winter-weight breeches are worn with cavalry issue boots. His German M1916 steel helmet displays the flaming skull emblem (**inset**) often seen on the headgear of the Horse Artillery. He is equipped with a German-made artillery rangefinder and a container for carrying shell fuses, as well as a Finnish-made tool kit.

## F: FINNISH HOME FRONT, 1941–44
### F1: First Lieutenant instructor, Civil Guard, Häme District

The German shoulder-fired, single-use Panzerfaust-klein and Panzerfaust-30 anti-tank rockets were provided in summer 1944; they were not nearly so popular and successful as the bazooka-based, reloadable Panzer-schreck launcher which was also supplied. This Civil Guard instructor wears on the sleeve of his m/36 tunic the Civil Guard arm shield, below badges identifying him as an instructor for boys' training schools. The SK emblem is repeated in brass on his pre-war green-piped shoulder straps, below crossed rifles. On his breast is a Reserve Officers School graduate's badge. His Czechoslovakian M1934 steel helmet has wire bent around it for the attachment of foliage camouflage.

### F2: Volunteer, Boys' Unit, Civil Guard

This teenager is a member of the youth section of the Civil Guard, whose members were known after 1941 as *Sotilaspojat* or 'soldier boys'. He wears a rather baggy light khaki cotton 'air raid suit', with Laplander boots. The insignia of the youth units is displayed on the left sleeve (**inset**). Note the reinforced elbows, and the fact that the black plastic buttons are concealed apart from the large one which fastens the waist band. His sidecap has the standard enlisted ranks' cockade on the front, and a black leather

chinstrap worn at the front in regulation style. His only equipment is the large leather despatch case in which he carries messages to the front line.

### F3: First Lieutenant, Frontier units

Frontier units fulfilled an important role in the Finnish military, and this young officer is far from being a 'second line' soldier. He wears standard m/36 winter uniform with straight-leg trousers, field cap and Laplander boots. On the shoulder straps of his tunic he dislays the distinctive brass bear's-head badge of the Frontier units. His equipment is a canvas 'bread bag' and a leather belt with Finnish-made ammunition pouches, and a pair of German binoculars. The Finnish-made m/28-30 Mosin-Nagant rifle was a sturdy and reliable weapon produced in the Civil Guard-owned SAKO factory.

## G: CONTINUATION WAR, 1941–44
### G1: Machine gun crewman, Infantry

As a member of the crew of a Soviet-designed M1910 Maxim HMG this private is carrying the metal ammunition case containing feed belts for his weapon, and is also weighed down with a wooden carrier for a spare barrel. Over his m/36 winter uniform he is wearing the enlisted man's greatcoat; note also the felt-and-leather winter boots. His personal equipment is limited to a water bottle, a hunting knife, and a Finnish-made canvas bandolier with spare clips for his ex-Soviet Mosin-Nagant M1891 rifle.

### G2: Lieutenant, Transport Corps

On the shoulder straps of his m/36 wool uniform this officer displays the brass winged wheel emblem of the Transport Corps (**inset**); dull metal rank roses are pinned directly to the collar. His boots are the less common type with strapped anklets. On his belt are canvas Soviet two-pocket ammunition

Two junior officers pose for the camera during the Continuation War. The left hand man wears the m/22 Army officer's greatcoat with its dark grey fall collar and cuffrings; the officer at the right has a double-breasted, fleece-lined short winter coats. Note that he wears straight-cut trousers, apparently with puttees and ankle boots. (Marshall Kregal Collection)

Continuation War: a mortar team pose for the camera in
typical summer uniforms, with German helmets camouflage-
painted for summer forest fighting. The junior sergeant on
the right is equipped with a map case and a Mauser
'broomhandle' pistol in a wooden shoulder stock/holster, as
well as his own antler-handled hunting knife. (Marshall
Kregal Collection)

pouches with spare clips for his captured Soviet M1938
carbine, which was a well-modernized version of the
M1891 model.

### G3: Lieutenant tank commander, Armoured Brigade/Division 'Lagus'

Armoured crewmen, like the cavalry, were often picked for
their small build to make it easier to move inside their tanks.
As with most armoured crewmen this young lieutenant wears
a mix of uniform items. His m/36 summer tunic has the black
collar patches of armoured troops, and on his right sleeve is
the badge of the armoured formation (**inset**). Black leather
tank breeches were issued to crewmen but were not always
worn, some favouring ordinary trousers. The canvas and
leather helmet is a captured Soviet item. His high officer's
boots are Finnish, as is the holster for his Czech VZ-24 semi-
automatic pistol.

## H: LAPLAND WAR, 1944–45
### H1: Private, Infantry

During the brief war with Germany the Finnish Army wore
basically unchanged uniforms, but this soldier's mixture of
clothing reflects late-war shortages. His long-obsolete
m/27 brown wool tunic is worn with a standard m/36 field
cap. The white camouflage over-trousers are worn over a
pair of m/36-cut winter trousers made from the same
brown cloth as the tunic, and are tucked into Laplander
boots. His weapon is a Finnish-made Mosin-Nagant m/28-
30 rifle, and he has its scabbarded bayonet on his belt.

### H2: Private, Infantry

This young recruit has been issued with a plain m/36 tunic,
straight-leg trousers and Laplander boots. His helmet is yet
another foreign import – a green-painted Swedish M1937, of
which the Finnish Army ordered 20,000 in June 1941. His
equipment includes a canvas rucksack, and an entrenching
tool in a leather carrier. Presumably the soldier is carrying
spare 'stick' magazines for his late-model Suomi kp/31 sub-
machine gun in his rucksack.

### H3: Captain, Infantry

His private purchase m/36 officer's tunic in this case displays
the infantry arm-of-service badge on the shoulder straps,
and on the left breast an array of medal ribbons identifying
his veteran status. His officer's quality sidecap has the
officer's badge and the green piping of the Infantry; its black
leather chin strap is worn at the front, as was the usual
practice. His belt is the brocade m/22 officer's full dress
type, with a polished brass buckle plate carrying the Finnish
lion symbol.

# INDEX